To: Sally with lots
of love from Aunt Louise
May this lovely book
help you to enjoy your
own "heavenly gardens".
                    5/27/2000

Happy Birthday

HEAVEN IN A WILD FLOWER

HEAVEN IN A

Wild Flower

SPIRITUAL REFLECTIONS

VERA GLENN

ILLUSTRATIONS BY ALICE HYVONEN

CHRYSALIS BOOKS

West Chester, Pennsylvania

©2000 by Vera Glenn

Library of Congress Cataloging-in-Publication Data
Glenn, Vera P.
  Heaven in a wild flower : spiritual reflections / Vera Glenn.
    p.   cm.
  Includes bibliographical references.
  ISBN 0-87785-392-4
    1. Glenn, Vera P.   2. Spiritual biography.   3. Gardening—Religious aspects.   4. Gardens—Religious aspects.   I. Title.

BL73.G54 A3 2000
242—dc21
                                                            99-087537

Edited by Betty Christiansen

Designed by Alice Hyvonen, Philadelphia, Pennsylvania

Illustrations on cover and in book by Alice Hyvonen are based on photographs of the author's garden, taken by Lucas Mergen.

Credit: The recipe for "Joe Froggers" (pp. 114–115) is reprinted with permission of the Publick House, Sturbridge, Massachusetts

Set in Stone Print Roman, Penumbra, and Vivaldi by Nesbitt Graphics, Glenside, Pennsylvania
Printed in the United States of America.

Chrysalis Books is an imprint of the Swedenborg Foundation Publishers. For more information, contact:

CHRYSALIS BOOKS
Swedenborg Foundation Publishers
320 N. Church Street
West Chester, Pennsylvania 19380
(610) 430-3222
Or
http://www.swedenborg.com

TO MY HUSBAND

BRUCE GLENN

WITH WHOM I HOPE TO LIVE IN AN ETERNAL GARDEN

CONTENTS

CONTENTS

ACKNOWLEDGMENTS

My deep appreciation goes to all those who have contributed to my love of growing things and to the garden itself, and so to the making of this book. Among many, I would like to mention specially my daughter Rachel, who was there from the beginning of the garden and the book; Lucas, my former student and a photographer, who gave me the pleasure of introducing him to the wildflowers and then took such beautiful portraits of them; two friends—Katie, my first and perhaps most enthusiastic reader, and Anne, a steady source of faith and encouragement. And my grateful thanks also goes to the helpful people at the Swedenborg Foundation.

One warm April day, there were bloodroots in full bloom, as if they had sprung out of hiding when my back was turned to shout, "Surprise!"

INTRODUCTION

WE SEE HUMAN THOUGHT AND FEELING BEST AND CLEAREST BY SEEING
IT THROUGH SOMETHING SOLID THAT OUR HANDS HAVE MADE.
EUDORA WELTY

Over the years, perhaps twenty or more, I have been making a wildflower garden behind a high hedge in my backyard. A long time before I came to live here, the space had been used to grow a few vegetables. Then, as the trees and shrubs grew up and made too much shade for string beans and tomatoes, it went to weeds. When I'm not around to tame it anymore, the place will probably revert back to wilderness. But while I live on this earth, it is a garden. What I have made with my hands (and heart) reflects clearly my own best thoughts and feelings, and perhaps those of others too, as Welty so well expresses.

In the preface to a tiny book, *Garden Proverbs*, Terry Berger, the editor, wrote this wonderful line:

> The garden is a metaphor for life itself.

Several months ago, I was having a conversation with another woman, and she asked me what I was doing now that I had retired from teaching. When I told her that I was writing a book about my wildflower garden, she said, "Well, I probably won't read it. I'm not a gardener." I replied, "Not a natural one, perhaps, but I think we're all spiritual gardeners."

Afterward, reflecting on the exchange, I admitted that gardening might not be for everyone. Others have their own metaphors for internal life according to their own special loves. The gardening metaphor suits me because I love gardening, and I can see many applications in planting and tending something growing to regeneration—the work of trying to become a better and more internally beautiful person. One of the reasons I find a garden such an apt analogy to life is that it is not ever made and done with, never fixed or "solid," but always changing and growing. I agree with Margery Bianco, an American horticulturist, who said,

> One of the best things about a garden, large or small, is that it is never finished. It is a continual experiment.

In the spring, dreams of how to refurbish the wildflower garden swim in my imagination. This is the creative part of gardening—the vision, the forming of the garden for the total effect. The weeding and the nurturing, of course, they are part of it, too. And the blooming, that is delightful. I love to walk through my gardens and enjoy each emerging leaf and flower. But as I walk about admiring, I'm always thinking of ways to change things. I'm grateful to be allowed to potter around reshaping God's creation, poking my fingers into divine business, taking advantage of the juice of life rising in the stems and stalks—having the joy of it.

In the summer, I put my energies into serious renovation: into weeding, rooting out, rearranging. I've always loved the process of renovation, of making something more attractive or more useful from what was lying around at hand. In the garden, I like working in an existing space with the preexisting conditions of shade and soil, with the plants that are already there as well as ones I bring in. I love to plan and lay out paths winding around trees already grown tall, and then, in a year or so, see a better way to go and make a new path. I like to make decisions between the weeds that must be thrown out and the weeds that are really flowers in disguise and can be invited to stay, or at least be left alone to see what will become of them.

Autumn, after the flowers are gone and the garden is reduced to trees and shrubs, could be compared to the beginning of a ripening age that brings clearer judgment and wisdom. At least, we get better at knowing what to cut out of our lives. When the excess of summer growth dies back, it is easier to see what is worth saving, which branch to prune and which to leave. We see a different beauty in what is spare and lean, in our life as in a garden. The coming on of winter is the gardener's friend, because it allows for some much-needed rest. And winter makes a clean sweep, gives opportunity, as it were, to start each spring fresh, from the ground up.

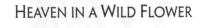

HEAVEN IN A WILD FLOWER

*Like a lot of foreigners, snowdrops loved American soil
and, having left the old world behind, flourished here.*

On the Winter Garden

JANUARY/FEBRUARY

WITH A GARDEN THERE IS HOPE.
GRACE FIRTH

It is cold and there is frost in the ground, but the sun shines stronger now than it did in December; there are more hours of daylight. The year has turned, and it is time to come with me into the wildflower garden.

The garden lies up the slight slope of back lawn from the kitchen door, tucked in under the low hill and so protected from the fiercest north winds. The way into the garden is through the old privet hedge on one of three narrow paths. This January morning the hedge is a-chirp with chickadees, scolding a little as I come through, but not too irately. These clever little blackcaps know who puts the sunflower seeds in the feeder round the side of the house. A squirrel scrambles away from me and up the trunk of the mulberry, makes an agile jump to the high wooden fence, and flees along the top, as if I was a threat to his existence instead of his benefactor. Of course, there are no leaves yet on the trees, or even buds swelling; the garden will not be shadowy for several months. Until then it is a sun trap, and on this sunny day anything seems possible. The snowdrops might be up.

The garden paths are deep in leaves, dumped there from the lawn raking in the fall and not yet rotted down. My daughter, Rachel, doesn't like walking on the paths in the winter because she's sure mice are hiding in the snug air pockets under the dead leaves. She doesn't want to tread on them. Our heavier snows, which usually come in February and March, will compress the leaves and flatten the mouse chambers—if there are any. As I walk through the garden, I pick up a few twigs and fallen branches strewn around by last week's storm. It is not yet time for a real cleanup, so the stroll toward the brush pile behind the garden shed with my handful of debris is only a token gesture of the work to come. In bending to pick up another dead stick, my eye is caught by a small clump of gray-green spears pushing up through the leaf mold just off the path. When I gently nudge aside the gray tatters of leaf ghosts with my fingers, the dark earth is very cold to my touch. But these spears are indeed the first leaves of the snowdrops. Although it is winter still, the growing season of my wildflower garden has begun.

Because SNOWDROPS are so prolific in my garden and all around Bryn Athyn, Pennsylvania, where I live, I was surprised when I went to look them up in my wildflower books not to find even a mention in the American guides. However, both my British books listed them. *The Ladybird Book of British Wild Flowers* said snowdrops were planted often in English gardens, but "very far from common" in the wilds. Yet on the last page of *The Observer's Book of Wild Flowers*, W. J. Stokoe, in a 1937 book that was reprinted in 1967, says that although the snowdrop is not indigenous to England, it has naturalized there very well. He has this description of it:

> Its rootstock takes the form of a little brown bulb, and from this appears . . . a solitary pair of long, straight-sided narrow leaves of a glaucous or sea-green color, and slightly keeled on the outer surface. A little later there comes up direct from the bulb an unbranched flower stem or scape, bearing a large bract or spathe, from which issues the solitary flower on a thin, bending stalk.

> The three sepals are pure white, and the three smaller petals are also white, but with a patch of green near the upper end of each. There are six stamens and a slender style. The flower is honeyed and scented, and remains open from about ten till four . . . flowering from January to March.

PAGE 216

4

So, snowdrops came to us from England, as did many of our early settlers along the eastern seaboard. But where they came from before that, Stokoe does not say. Did a bulb or two tuck away in one of the boats from Jutland that raided the English coast? Or perhaps come home in the pocket of a crusader? I suppose I could search out the answer in some botanical tome, but I think I would rather speculate. However the flower got to the British Isles, it was Anglicized there and arrived in this country with English habits, and so fit in right away, at least in southeastern Pennsylvania. Like a lot of foreigners, snowdrops loved American soil and, having left the old world behind, flourished here.

In England, in another January, Edith Holden, an amateur naturalist, wrote in her 1906 journal:

> Primroses, Polyanthus, Winter Aconite. Mazereon and
> Snowdrops are all in flower in the garden. Every mild morning
> now the birds are singing and they continue more or less
> throughout the day.
>
> **PAGE 9**

The facsimile of Edith Holden's 1906 journal was just published in 1977, as *The Country Diary of an Edwardian Lady.* My husband Bruce gave it to me as my gift book at Christmas. What a delightful collection of observations of flowers and birds in the English countryside, and charming watercolor illustrations by the author, interspersed with verses and sayings about nature through the months. Both Bruce and I loved to walk out in nature, often with the children, to see what we could see and discover what was blooming. But we didn't have a chance to ramble almost every day as the Edwardian lady did. How wonderful it would be to have the wildflowers close at hand, where we could keep an eye on their comings and goings. Holden's book was an inspiration. And so began the idea of making the wild garden, which I started the next spring.

It wasn't until several years after the garden became a reality that I started to keep a journal of my experiences. In 1985, my friend Anne, very much an Edwardian lady herself, gave me a book for my birthday called *Nature Notes*, with selected quotations and illustrations from Holden's *Diary* and dated spaces for my own nature observations. I made that book last two years by using two colors of ink: blue for one year and green for the next. If I didn't write something every day, I felt incomplete. Writing regularly honed my powers of both observation and reflection as I tried to describe accurately what I saw and record what meaning it had in my life. After two years, writing in a journal became such a habit that it has continued to the present, and I have filled many other blank books. One or two of these books included pertinent quotations about gardening, which I took to heart. A number of the quotations are happily incorporated into these pages.

When I came to write about my wildflower garden, my journals were invaluable. They refreshed my memories and brought back the sense of immediacy that makes the experience live again. Here, for example, are some entries from my January journals about snowdrops:

1986

JANUARY 1

Like noses poking from a winter blanket, the tips of snowdrop leaves are just emerging in our wildflower garden. It is early, but December has been so mild. On our walk yesterday along the driveway, through the Cairncrest woods, Bruce and I found the snowdrops pushed up an inch or two higher than ours, but no white showing yet. They always bloom first on this hillside. Location seems to make such a difference in the timing of the blossoms, sometimes as much as two weeks. I wouldn't think that the plants would get more sun here than in our garden, but perhaps it is the somewhat higher elevation.

1991

JANUARY 24

Sighting the first snowdrops along the Cairncrest drive has become a pleasant neighborhood contest that turns a winter afternoon's walk into a pilgrimage. Our friends the Woodards, who often walk that way, say that the plants are well up and showing white, but not yet in bloom.

JANUARY 25

The report from our neighbor down the road is that the Cairncrest snow-drops are in full flower.

JANUARY 26

I checked out those snowdrops for myself yesterday, and my version is that they are more than tight buds, but not yet fully open.

JANUARY 29

The snowdrops in the Glenn wildflower garden are still in the pushing-up-out-of-the-earth stage—gray-green spears of leaves, white and pale-green striped buds showing between the leaves, very tight and low to the earth. Today's warmth and tomorrow's promised rain may bring them into a more open state, but I wouldn't want to rush them. To know that they are coming is enough to keep hope springing. In these days of winter's discontent, I realize how much the garden means to me; even picking up a few sticks and throwing them on the compost pile makes me feel more cheerful.

1994

JANUARY 28

It has been a horrible month of snow, sleet, and freezing rain. Everything is covered in ice. It struck me as I was trying to chop a channel in my glacier with a rusty hatchet—to drain off the water from the heavy rain and melting snow instead of having it pour down the incline into my basement—that in other winters the snowdrops would be well up, proba-bly blooming along the Cairncrest drive, or even in my wildflower garden. Is it worth it to struggle up the icy slope of the lawn to the garden to look?

JANUARY 30

Amazing! Where it has melted a little in the garden, the snowdrops are pushing up through the frozen earth and icy leaf mold. Those hardy shoots that come as an early promise of spring are urging me to begin to tune my ear for birdsong and frog peep, set my nose for odor of wet loam, and turn my back on this grim January.

After the miserable, icy weeks of early 1994, the world was still wintry at the end of March. A trip south—even a little bit south to visit my stepson David and his family in Maryland—seemed like it might offer some more positive glimpse of spring. I wanted to bring a gift of flowers because my little granddaughter Elizabeth loved my gardens and any kind of flower. The daffodils were only buds. The snowdrops were past their prime, but pretty in a faded way, so I dug several clumps to plant in their backyard for next year. Maryland wasn't warm and sunny, as I'd hoped; the weather seemed a lot like home. In spite of it, three children and I trooped out enthusiastically to dig holes in the impacted earth and stuff in the snowdrop bulbs. The last went in in the cold rain. At home a few days later, I wrote in my journal that "the brightest part of the weekend was planting snowdrops with the children in the tiny backyard, while the toddler watched from the window, confined to the house so he wouldn't get wet and muddy."

All of the snowdrops in my garden—and there is an abundance—grew from a few bulbs brought home from school in a paper drinking cup by my first grader. That very morning, Rachel told me excitedly, their teacher had taken them to visit her beautiful garden. For my little daughter, it had been a morning in fairyland. The teacher had shown them lots of wildflowers and told them all the names, which Rachel couldn't remember; they'd had their snack in the picnic place by the pool, with real goldfish, and then been allowed to run free along the paths through the flowery woods. The steep path down to the shallow creek was banked higher than the children's heads with azaleas of every delicious color.

Then, before they walked the third of a mile back to the classroom, the teacher had given them a little flower or a few bulbs to take home and plant in their own gardens. The white cup was grimy and crumpled in the middle from being held tightly all the way in Rachel's small hand. Inside were four or five muddy white-and-brown bulbs, their narrow leaves drooping over the top of the cup.

What flowers were left were frayed and gray; most had gone to the smooth, green, oval seed pod. They did not look very promising to me. But after lunch, we took a trowel and went out back to where I was beginning to make a wildflower garden and planted the bulbs. The leaves splayed out on the ground. By the time the school year ended in June, there wasn't a trace of them.

The snowdrops were hardier than they seemed; they did appear the next January and even bloomed. Before long, the few single bulbs proliferated into many tight clumps of spear-like leaves and delicate-looking white flowers. When a clump of snowdrops becomes overcrowded, like a teeming tenement, the larger bulbs at the bottom push out the smaller ones. After the flowering is over and the leaves die down, you can often see the bulbs lying in heaps on the top of the ground. I suppose that heavy rains, birds, and small animals move these rejects around to uninhabited locations, where they settle in and begin to grow new colonies. When they get entrenched, there is no stopping them. In a few years, I was digging up snowdrops to give away, and even to throw away, although the bulbs usually outmaneuver me and grow wherever I dump them.

Snowdrops are amazing flowers. In their white bonnets, the "fair maids of February," as someone named them, are tough cookies. They push up through the frost-bound soil, and once up, the harshest weather does not daunt them. The "winter flower," one of my students called it in a little poem she wrote for a creative writing class years ago. She compared the snowdrop to a woman, pure and modest, yet strong enough to stand up through the vicissitudes of the climate, even though so fragile in appearance. I've thought often about that poem. If I had a copy of it now, I would love to include it here, with her permission. Instead, I'll substitute a portion of another poem about the snowdrop, which expresses something of the same idea:

> One month is past, another is begun,
> Since merry bells rang out the dying year,
> And buds of rarest green began to peer,

As if impatient for a warmer sun;
And though the distant hills are bleak and dun,
The virgin snowdrop, like a lambent fire,
Pierces the cold earth with its green-streaked spire.

HARTLEY COLERIDGE, FEBRUARY 1, 1842

With my husband's physical death from cancer at the end of May in 1992, I almost gave up the wildflower garden. There were external reasons, but perhaps the most pervasive was my own winter state of mental and physical inertia. I was very tired. There had been three months of intensive nursing when I only infrequently found a moment to visit the garden, and did not have time or energy to work there. The feeling of indifference to what had previously brought me such joy dragged on like a long cold spell. At some point, a widowed friend said to me, "In a year or two, when the grief eases a little, you will find that you rejoice in the spring again."

And so I do. I find in the garden, and perhaps especially in the winter garden, the rejuvenation of natural and spiritual life. As in the snowdrop, the lambent fire was only temporarily banked down under the frozen earth; the human spirit is strong to live and grow, although it may sometimes seem to be dead and buried.

By the middle of February, if the weather has been mild, the wildflower garden is a drift of white. I can see the snowy mounds through the sparse winter hedge from my kitchen window, and so enjoy the bloom inside as well as out. By the end of the month, the pale lavender crocus will be adding a touch of color to the garden and throughout the lawn.

1988

FEBRUARY 29

The snow has gone at last and left behind along the edge of the ivy at the front of the house a fringe of early crocus blooms. Crocuses are always a surprise, springing up in the lawn before I expect them, before any real warmth has come to the earth. They have a fresh scent, rather nose-tickling, but sweet enough to entice out the first bee.

1990

FEBRUARY 26

It was eight degrees above zero this morning. I shiver for the vegetation and the crocuses that pushed out into bud and bloom with such cheerful expectation in the warm days earlier in the week.

FEBRUARY 28

Snow fell heavily for about two hours yesterday afternoon. With drooping heads and limp leaves, the crocuses look as if they had been punished. Crocuses do not fare as well in stormy weather as snowdrops. Sleet tears holes in their petals and wet snow lays their heads on the ground, from which slaughter they do not rise. But while they last, they are the happiest of flowers.

1997

FEBRUARY 19

There is the most delightful marching line of crocus children in the sunshine by the front door today. The sight makes me think of the parade of the flowers, an illustration in The Root Children *by Sibylle von Olfers. I haven't seen the book for years, but I loved it as a child.*

FEBRUARY 27

The crocuses are closed up against the rain this morning. They look like furled umbrellas. Give us just a touch of sun, and they will open like tiny parasols.

The CROCUS belongs to the family *Iridaceae*, to which the iris also belongs. There is a variety of crocuses in bright colors: purple, yellow, red-orange, and white, the pale lilac, and even striped and veined ones. They grow in tufts of grassy foliage from underground corms. Most bloom gaily in the spring, but there are also autumn crocuses. The variety I have had blooming in the front yard for years and now in the wildflower garden is, I think, the *Crocus vernus* or spring crocus. It is lavender and very early blooming, even before true spring. It looks to my eye much like the *Crocus zonatus* that blooms in the fall. Both naturalize well if you leave the plant to mature and do not cut down the foliage too soon. This leaves the lawn looking shaggy for a while, but it's worth it for next February's bloom.

Because they act like wildflowers, I tried planting the shaggy little bulbs in the wildflower garden, but for years they didn't do well. Why something grows prolifically in one place and not another is often a mystery. Perhaps even the leafless branches of the garden trees made more shade than they liked. However, the sight of crocuses spilling all down one long open slope and into the woods on my friend Katie's shady property renewed my determination to try again. Katie offered to let me dig some new bulbs from their grounds. And this year, I was rewarded with many blooms out in the wildflower garden, either because of the new, hardier strain of crocus or a different, sunnier location.

In fact, there have never been so many early crocuses blooming everywhere as there are this year. There is one house in Bryn Athyn that has them cascading down a steep bank and out across the lawn in such profusion that the ground is solid lavender. It is such a show that cars driving along the street slow down to look. I see these little crocuses popping up around the area in other places where I have never noticed them before, and I wonder, how did they get there? They don't fly through the air like winged seeds; they aren't eaten and dropped by birds or buried by squirrels. When I'm digging, I do find small progeny near a mature corm parent, which shows how crocuses spread in their immediate location, but how to account for such widespread distribution? Magic!

Just a spring ago, I planted out in the wild garden a rooted cutting from my old Pussy Willow (*Salix discolor*) by the house. That tree is doing poorly, so I'm trying to get another one started. I can't imagine living through February without those soft, furry catkins to console me. When the brown shells first split and drop away, the kittens clinging to the supple branches are sleek and gray. Then they fluff out, at first white, then covered in tiny blooms thick with yellow pollen. The leaves of this shrublike tree come later. They are smooth below and toothed above the middle, elliptical, and whitish underneath, and much enjoyed by Japanese beetles.

1996

FEBRUARY 25

On the dogwoods' lateral branches, the little gray knobs of buds are standing up to be counted. This dormant period sometimes tries the patience, but as long as there are a few encouraging signs—curls of crocus, soft pussies on the willow, new minted green of tiny celandine leaves, and the red bloom on the maple—then, I can wait for the glory burst of flowering that is surely coming.

The periwinkle had been green all winter, and now, in spring, the lavender-blue pinwheels, with stars outlined in white in their centers, were showing up among the leaves.

My Secret Garden

MAKING A GARDEN, NO MATTER HOW SIMPLE, IS A CREATIVE ENDEAVOR
AND IT SHOULD RELATE TO THE PERSON WHO OWNS IT AND BE IN
SOME WAY A CONSCIOUS EXPRESSION OF [HERSELF].
NANCY GRASBY

The old Pennsylvania farmhouse of stucco-covered stone, my childhood home, still stands on a rise of ground at the end of a long gravel lane. In those far-off days when I was young, there was a path running from the back porch of the farmhouse to the vegetable garden, then on down the slope, across the plank bridge to the spring-house door, and up the steep bank into the apple orchard on the far hill. When little more than a toddler, I used to go into the vegetable garden with my mother, where she pulled weeds or harvested early lettuce and radishes. From the rows of beets and carrots, it was only a wander away down to the little creek we called "the stream," and to imaginative adventure. This clear stream of water runs through my early memories. Growing up is symbolized by moving my play farther and farther down stream away from the house and my mother's watchful eye at the kitchen window.

At the bottom of the bank, I found a little island near the plank bridge. It was made by the running stream on one side and the languid course of the overflow from the springhouse on the other. In the quiet water warmed by the sun, watercress grew bright green before the cold of March was gone. Because I knew that she liked it, I'd pull some to take up to my mother. There were sometimes tiny black snails on the leaves that had been underwater, and once I found an orange salamander caught in the muddy roots. Mother would wash the cress and put it in a bowl as a salad for our dinner. I was never sure if I liked it; it was so peppery on the tongue.

For a while, that island became my moated grange. The elder-berry bushes that grew there made a roof; their stems divided the house into rooms that I could just squeeze into, or smaller crevices where I stored things. One spring day, I brought my kindergarten sweetheart, Bobby, to my island, which he thought was neat. But when I explained the game—I would be the mother, he would be the daddy, and two of my dolls would be our children—Bobby refused to cooperate. My proposed innocent afternoon in the Garden of Eden was spoiled. I could play house if I wanted to, but he was going home. And he did.

Like the stream, I moved along—away from the shelter of the springhouse, to an open stretch between grassy banks. I only invited girls to play now. Much inspired by the study of American Indian culture in second grade, we made pots out of the clay from the banks and baked them in the hot sun. We were hunters and gatherers of weeds and flowers, concocting messes in Mother's cast-off pans that we never dared to eat, dying scraps of cloth—and our hands—from the juice of pokeberries or black walnut husks. We built dams of stones that we lifted, straining, out of the stream bed, caught crayfish, were scared by the striped garter snakes slithering through the tall grass.

Third-grade summer, we played mostly out of sight of the farmhouse, except for glimpses of the roof above the sweet black cherry tree. Mother would sometimes come around the big clump of lilacs at the end of the lawn to see what we were up to. We had found, down below the raspberry patch, a small pool by a shelving granite rock. Our efforts to build dams had been puny, but this one had been made by a grown-up, by Mr. Boxton, a black man who lived in the two-room shack downstream, on the other side from the old farmhouse. His shack had no running water, so Mr. Boxton made the pool so that he could dip his water buckets full. On summer days when he was away in his rattly wooden-slatted truck, we used his water hole to wade, and splash, and even try to paddle a little. He must have been less than pleased, coming home at the end of a hot day of working in the sun, to find his water source all muddied up.

From the pool, we plunged on into the shadows of the woods of black walnut trees, spicebushes, and tangled honeysuckle vines that grew on the banks. We explored the stream bed, where we could no longer be seen, reached only by the sound of the cowbell summoning us home. One spring, when I was about ten or eleven—old enough to read *The Secret Garden* and revel in the idea of a girl finding her own secret place and working to make it bloom and flourish—I discovered a spot along the stream I'd never seen before. I had been walking down the grassy track below the oldest apple orchard. In the underbrush along the stream bank, I noticed a faint path leading in toward the water, trodden by animals—probably thirsty groundhogs coming down from their burrows among the rows of thick gray apple trunks on the bluff above me. Following the animal path into the thicket, I slipped on the earth of the steep bank and skidded down into a small green valley the stream had cut. At the upper end was a little waterfall, and maybe twenty yards downstream, the water slid smoothly out and away around a bend. The stream coming at flood over the big gray rock had scoured a coarse sand beach below the falls. The rest of the verge was covered with silky grass, fine as baby's hair. Grass grew, but also some rank weeds, and here and there a blackberry bramble thrust through. Near the curve of the stream, where the water ran very quietly, sprouted a bunch of late daffodils, bright yellow.

A few days later, I brought my cousin Laddie there and shared the secret with her. The daffodils made us both see the potential of the place as a garden—our special woodland garden. The rest of that spring and into the summer, we worked spasmodically to make it so, pulling weeds and scratching ourselves digging out briars. We retrieved more daffodil bulbs from further upstream where Mr. Boxton had dumped the refuse from his landscaping business. We transplanted violets and spring beauties from the orchard. We wove a gate of honeysuckle and branches across the stream at the lower end of the garden to completely enclose us. And sometimes, we just sat and watched the water running down the big rock by ferny crevices, making brown bubbles that hurried away below the waterfall.

Flowing water and years bring changes. Laddie and I got into our teens and grew out of playing by the stream. When I went back several seasons later, to the place that had once seemed so special, the magic and the daffodils were gone. There was no garden. The once-sparkling stream was now only a trickle of water; the banks all overgrown with poison ivy and sumac. Nothing is perfect except a vision and a memory.

Perhaps it was to recreate the memory of that secret garden of my childhood that I started to make a wildflower garden in the wasteland behind the privet hedge of my married home many years later. For happy childhood experiences remain with us, and from these innocent affections, we build our spiritual places.

In thinking back, I realize that although I enjoyed nature and flowers from the time I was a little girl, my desire to be a gardener didn't really flourish until I had a home and gardens of my own. Even tending the garden along the stream was more playacting out a book I had loved than real gardening. Working in the family vegetable garden or among Mother's flowers didn't engage my affections very deeply. There is such a difference between gardening because it is a task set for you by your mother, and gardening because you are responsible for the garden and want it to be beautiful and abundant—not to impress the neighbors with a weed-free appearance or Miracle-Gro results, but to satisfy something in yourself. The more care and attention I give a garden, the more of myself I put into helping plants root and blossom, fruit and bear seed, the more the garden becomes my own, and the more I love it.

A friend of mine whose husband grew beautiful roses once told me that she wasn't content just working in her husband's gardens. In truth, she said, he didn't really require her help. She needed a garden of her own to care for. She had started several around their property, but as her husband found new varieties of roses to try, his gardens expanded and took over. I'm sure that he didn't realize that he was growing beauty at the expense of his wife's need. If he had, he would have willingly given her a place to make for herself the garden she so much wanted.

Each of us humans, perhaps a woman particularly, needs something like a garden in which to grow her creative talents and work out the story of her inner life. This was the underlying theme of a novel by Elizabeth von Arnim called *Elizabeth and Her German Garden*. Married to a man who took her to live far from her family and her country on an isolated estate in Prussia, this woman would have perished if she hadn't had a garden.

We grow to love the people and pets that we nurture. I don't feel at all tolerant of the nasty habits of my neighbors' cats and dogs, yet I've even become fond of the squirrels that munch up the sunflower seeds I put out for chickadees and cardinals. Because I sustain them through the winter, they are my squirrels. I believe that we love our children, at least partly, because we have fed them so many peanut-butter sandwiches, bundled them in snowsuits to keep them warm, rescued them before they fell and skinned their knees, or, if we didn't get there in time, kissed the hurt place and put on a Band-Aid. Our children respond to life more fully because of our tending, and we respond to life more fully because of tending them.

I believe it is the same with gardens. We care for our flowers, because we care for them. As Saint-Exupery wrote in *The Little Prince*, "It is the time you have wasted for your rose that makes your rose so important."

Before he married me in July 1968, Bruce, as a widower with five children, hadn't had time to do much with the yard except mow grass and rake leaves. There was a rather desultory rock garden on the bank at the front of the house and an old peace rosebush at the corner, but most of the property was open, with a few trees and shrubs. Bruce replanted the rock garden on Good Friday of the year we were courting. The resuscitation of this garden was symbolic for him of new beginnings. From then on, it became an annual ritual of ours to work together on the property at Eastertide—clearing away the dead debris of winter, rejoicing in the burst of crocuses from the cold ground, and planting bright-faced pansies. This was as much a celebration of our Lord's resurrection for us as going to church.

After my marriage, I continued to teach English and history at the Academy of the New Church Girls School situated in Bryn Athyn, Pennsylvania. I stopped teaching just before our second Christmas together, when my daughter, Rachel, was born, and I didn't pick it up again until ten years later. In the meantime, a son, Thane, was added to the family. With our two small children and two teenagers—David and Cara, the youngest of Bruce's first family—living with us, I was a busy mother. But I determined that when Thane was old enough not to need watching every moment, I would do two creative things: I would learn to bake bread, and I would start my very own garden.

Baking bread came first, because it was an in-house activity that went along with my already-established role of nourishing the family. I chose a recipe that my friend Katie had put in a community cookbook called *Rational Recipes: What's Cooking with the Bryn Athyn Women's Guild*. This recipe—Katie's mother's—is the one I still use today, though I have reduced it to two loaves from six.

MARGARETHA DAVIS' BROWN BREAD

1 pound brown sugar	3 packages yeast
1 egg	1/2 cup lukewarm water
6 teaspoons salt	1 teaspoon white sugar
1 tablespoon vegetable oil	about 6 cups white flour
8 cups whole-wheat flour	6 cups lukewarm water

Soak the yeast in the half-cup water to soften; sprinkle with white sugar. In a large bowl combine the brown sugar, egg, salt, oil, and whole-wheat flour. Slowly stir in the six cups of water. Add the softened yeast. Mix well. Add white flour until the dough pulls away from the sides of the bowl. Turn it out on a floured board. Knead, lightly rolling it in the palms of the hands. More flour may be added until the ball of dough no longer sticks to the hands.

Put the ball of dough back in the bowl, cover it, and let it rise until doubled. Turn it out on the board and cut it into six chunks. Knead each lightly, then shape them into loaves. Put them into greased pans and let them rise again. Bake in a 300-degree preheated oven about an hour or until they sound hollow when rapped.

I have good memories of going home with Katie, mid-afternoon after a college class, and finding her house filled with the delicious, yeasty smell of bread not long out of the oven. She'd call up the back-stairs to Mrs. Davis, who was resting, "Mama, may we cut a loaf of the bread?" Her mother's voice would come back, apologizing that it wasn't as good as usual, but go ahead. Then, we'd sit down at the kitchen table and gorge ourselves on thick, buttery slices while we talked over the excitements and traumas of college life.

I like to think that, along with making bread, I've made happy memories like these by baking for my children and others. The smell and taste of warm, baked things are associated with family and love, and they foster some of our most comforting feelings and reflections, as well as nourish our bodies.

I wouldn't have missed this homely act of natural good. It came in the right sequence. But having mastered brown bread, and with Thane being of a fairly reliable age, it was time to realize the second of my projects—making a garden for nourishing my spirit.

So one fine day in March 1978, I put on my gardening gloves; took a spade, clippers, and pruning shears; left house and children behind (temporarily); and set off across the backyard to challenge the wilderness. My destination was a strip of land at the end of our property, roughly seventy by thirty feet (as paced off unreliably by my size nines). Early on, Bruce had planted hedges to outline the perimeter of his property at the rear, and to separate his vegetable garden from the slope of back lawn. I think his brother, who was in landscaping, had given him a lot of leftover privet bushes. On the lawn side, which got the sun, the hedge had grown high, matured, and bent almost double with age. The space behind it was effectively screened from our house, if not so well from the neighbors.

There are no such things as coincidences, I believe. The same day I started the wild garden was the day that Homer, our neighbor to the west started to build a fence around his property. It was a homemade fence, an original design of woven boards between strong uprights, the wood left to weather. Before Homer made the fence, the border between our two properties was wide open, except for a sprawl of forsythia bushes roughly in line with the front of the hedge. Homer said he was putting up the fence so that they could put his daughter's dog outside without tying it up. I suspect that he was also protecting his vegetable garden from encroaching rabbits and giving his wife the chance to bend over with impunity in the asparagus patch. But whatever his reasons, the fence served my purpose famously. It enclosed my future garden on the western side, making it more private and woodsy.

On the eastern side of my retreat was a grassy building lot that sloped away to a quiet street. Children sometimes played in this field, but that was no problem, and the field was partly screened by a copse of bushes and scrubby trees that had grown up around the pole that rayed out electric and phone wires to our area. At the bottom of the metal brace for the pole was the cornerstone that marked the point where three properties met: ours, the neighbors' to the north, and the field, where there would someday be a house.

The biggest problem was along that north side of our yard, at the back where the old privet hedge had gotten scrawny, suffering from lack of light under a mulberry and a Norway maple that had grown up right on the property line. If I happened to be quietly working on the garden when the pretty teenage daughter came out to sunbathe in her yard, I felt uncomfortably like one of the elders spying on Suzanna. Thickening up the shrubbery along the boundary between the back neighbors and me seemed to be a priority for everyone's privacy. At first, I envisioned a bank of flourishing rhododendrons and azaleas, but somehow that never materialized. It wasn't just a matter of the expense, although we didn't have much money to spare on hired labor, nursery plants, and topsoil; it was the conviction that a wild garden shouldn't be a commercial enterprise. Instead, I dug up seedlings and rootlings from around the yard and transplanted them out back: an azalea or two that had layered, a holly, a pine, a yew. Once, in a fit of zeal, I singlehandedly dug up a four-foot spruce and lugged it to the back in a wheelbarrow, dug another hole, tipped it in, and tamped earth around it. The abused tree stayed green long enough to fool a bird into building a nest in it and then expired. Nothing really flourished in that sucked-out area among the roots of the big trees. The hedgerow never materialized.

Years and years after the garden was well established, the sparse screen continued to keep the garden from being really secluded along the back. I'd look at the gaps and wish we had gone ahead, hired a landscaper, and done it right. This was especially so when new neighbors moved in with lots of noisy children and two big dogs. The thin hedge perished completely as grass clippings, leaves, and other trash engulfed it. Before long, quite a mound of debris built up, which slid down into my garden.

1993

FEBRUARY 20

It was milder today. I picked up fallen twigs and branches in the wildflower garden to ready it for the blooming. The snowdrops are up, and other bulbs are pushing green leaves through the leaf mold. But it's not as peaceful out there as I'd like—the dogs bark at me if they are out in their yard and even bound across the line to tell me in no uncertain terms that I am encroaching on their preserve. I'm also getting tired of picking up rotting jack-o'-lanterns, ratty lime-green tennis balls, and pressed cardboard flower pots with dried stems sticking out of their parched soil. Sometimes I feel if I had just a bit more gumption I'd call and complain. Perhaps we could go together on a fence between the properties.

When I wrote that journal entry, I was in the doldrums and definitely didn't have the energy to raise a fuss. Anyway, it was winter, and I wasn't in the garden very much. So I thought I'd wait and see what the spring brought. It made me sad to think about it, but if things didn't get better, I might have to give up my wildflower garden.

But one day in early spring, I saw this neighbor out along the back line and plucked up my courage to go out and ask him if he thought anything could be done to improve the situation. Did he think, maybe, we should put up a fence? While we were standing there talking about it, his dogs rushed into my garden, barking at me ferociously. That cinched it. He was furious over their behavior and dragged them off by their collars into the house. He called me a few minutes later on the phone and said if that was what I had to put up with, no wonder I wanted a fence. It would definitely go up, and he would pay for most of it. So I got my garden back, secure behind a wooden wall, and I do believe, at least in this case, that a good fence does keep us good neighbors. Alluding here to Robert Frost's poem "Mending Wall" reminds me of another saying of Frost's that sums up the situation very neatly:

> Nature does not complete things. She's chaotic. Man must
> finish, and he does so by making a garden and building a wall.

Just a spring after the back fence went up, my neighbor poked his head over it one day while I was working quietly in the wildflower garden and asked, "Do you like the fence?" I told him I loved it, but how did he feel? He said he liked it too, and then added wistfully, "Your garden is so peaceful." Thanks to the fence, it had returned to tranquility.

But that very first morning in 1978, when I went out to make a garden, the area was anything but orderly and peaceful. It was more like a war zone. I slashed and dug, pulled and piled. It was tremendous fun. The maker of a garden, unlike the maker of a poem, doesn't often start with a clean page. There are usually things cluttering up the area that have to be gotten rid of before one can properly begin. This site was certainly no exception. After Bruce abandoned it as a vegetable garden, the patch grew up to weeds; it became an out-of-the-way place to dump the old swing set and burn the trash from the wastepaper baskets—some of which wasn't burnable. (Like an archaeologist on a dig, I still turn up the detritus of a past civilization: ancient bits of crockery and glass, headless plastic red Indians and yellow cowboys, fragments of old games, and, less interesting, the crushed, blackened scraps of aluminum trays from ready-to-heat meals.)

I was scratched and sweaty, but quite cheerful, when Bruce came out to see if I wanted to knock off for lunch. He said he'd gotten his freshman papers corrected, and he offered to help me a little in the afternoon, if I wanted. In truth, for all my exuberant efforts, not a very large space had been cleared. Besides, I didn't wish to be like Eve in Milton's *Paradise Lost*, who set off willfully to work by herself in the Garden of Eden and fell under the seduction of the serpent. So I gratefully accepted the masculine assistance of my Adam for the heaviest jobs and basked in his appreciation of my endeavors.

After lunch, the rest of the household came out to see the work in progress and stayed to help. The little children carefully put the bits and pieces of nonbiodegradable rubbish I'd collected into a plastic bag and carried it to our garbage can by the kitchen door. Cara discovered, back in the weeds, the low chicken wire enclosure that she and her best friend (the older sister of the sunbather) had built as a kitten farm long ago. The two little entrepreneurs started their venture with three kittens someone was giving away. They planned to raise the cats, then sell them to the neighbors and make a lot of money. Like many a childhood dream, this one didn't materialize, mostly because around here, one can't even give cats away. After a moment of nostalgia, Cara pulled up the stakes, bundled up the chicken wire, and carried it all away. My husband, with David's help, hefted the broken and rusted bars of the swing set, trailing vines to the roadside, where we hoped the trash collector would do his job. Then Bruce came back to clear a space behind the garden shed where he could build an incinerator out of the heap of cinder blocks left over from the construction of the addition to the house. This incinerator, he assured me, was meant only for brush and leaves that we didn't want in the compost pile—no more rubbish burning.

It was good to have the support of my family, for after all, it is really only an appearance that one does anything completely by oneself. In his theological books, Emanuel Swedenborg, the eighteenth-century scientist, philosopher, and revelator, calls this appearance the "as-of-self," because we function as if what we do is done by our own power. And it is an important appearance. The child's "I can do it myself" is what starts the whole process of growing up, and it pushes us to achievement all through life. But if we're rational about it, we see that everything we do depends on what other people contribute to the process. Whether it's the flour we put into bread or the sonnet form we use in writing a poem, someone else had a hand or a mind in it. And ultimately, everything comes to us from the Creator—life itself. So, although I started out with a great surge of "as-of-self" in making the wildflower garden, from that first day, others were part of the process, even if they only encouraged and enjoyed.

Wisely, no one ever tried to take the responsibility for the garden away from me. It was always my garden—the children called it "Mother's Secret Garden." The real secret garden, which of course my family didn't realize (and I didn't either for a long time) was the one that I was making inside myself while I was gardening. As I later wrote in a journal entry, "The deeper satisfaction of gardening that restores the spirit comes when you are working on something of your own—the secret garden of the soul."

By mid-April, putting in the odd hour here and there, I had finished clearing a fairly large area and laid out a path that ran from the opening in the middle of the privet hedge in a loop to the garden shed at the far right. Two kinds of plants that I had found growing vigorously were allowed to remain. English ivy had crept in along the back line, making an acceptable border of dark green. To the left of the path was a patch of PERIWINKLE or MYRTLE that Bruce had set out after the demise of the vegetable garden, hoping it would spread into a ground cover. It was slowly doing its job. The glossy, pointed leaves had been evergreen all winter, and now, in spring, the lavender-blue pinwheels, with stars outlined in white in their centers, were showing up among the leaves.

PERIWINKLE (*Vinca minor*). *Vincio* is Latin, meaning "to bind." *Vinca* means a band or what is bound. Use of the word in the identification refers to the long, supple stems with their leaves paired on either side like the wreaths or bands on the heads of Roman statues. I found out by looking it up in *A Field Guide to Wildflowers* by Roger Tory Peterson and Margaret McKenny that periwinkle is a member of the dogbane family. I wonder where that appellant came from? The dogbanes are closely related to the milkweeds and have the same milky fluid in the stems. Was this juice smeared on clothing to ward off fierce dogs or used to cure dog bites? Such a pretty plant and flower seem to deserve a better name.

Though the perimeters of the cleared space were still scruffy, there was no way that I could turn the whole area into a garden all at once. My garden plan was to start small. But that first year, I wanted something that I could set out right away to make a little show of color, so we decided to buy a few plants. Then, I would see what plants I could find growing wild in the woods, in the orchard around my childhood home, and along the roadsides. I would bring them home. If they didn't flourish, I'd try other things. Another source of plants that I didn't expect was generous gardeners, who gave me gifts from their own woods and gardens.

My garden design was very casual. It should be natural, I thought. It should look as if it came about innocently and artlessly. I'm not sure that I've ever been able to create the lovely, spontaneous, natural effect I hoped for, but no gardener was ever more innocent—or more ignorant, either, for that matter. When someone heard that I was going to write a book about my garden, she asked enthusiastically if I was going to tell her what wildflowers to grow and how. This woman would do better to turn to the work of a horticulturist. It is with a great sense of inadequacy that I realize I have no in-depth knowledge of soils and habitats, no expertise on plant varieties, on propagation and growing habits—nothing of value to pass on to others except experience and delight. The whole garden has been a hands-on experiment with some success, some failure, lots of hard work, and much enjoyment.

*Under the dark trees, the trilium glow with their own
brightness, as if each flower were a three-pointed star.*

THE GARDEN
OF THE
LORD

My wildflower garden was at least a dream in my mind before I became its gardener, but I think the reference above is to the biblical story of creation. The garden made before gardeners is the Garden of Eden—perhaps the most well-known garden in all of Western culture and no less important because it is allegorical. This garden created by God is on one level an earthly paradise, but on another level, I believe, it was and is symbolic of the human mind and its spiritual potential, "full of wisdom and perfect in beauty" (Ezekiel 28:12).

> The Lord God planted a garden eastward in Eden. . . . And out of the ground the Lord God made every tree grow that is pleasant to the sight and good for food. The tree of life in the midst of the garden, and the tree of the knowledge of good and evil.
>
> **GENESIS 2:8-9**

> Then the Lord God took the man and put him in the garden of Eden to tend and keep it.
>
> **GENESIS 2:15**

But Adam and his wife, as representatives of all humankind, couldn't keep it. Discontented with a life of simple perfection, they

31

were tempted to try what was forbidden. In aspiring to be like gods, they willfully determined to taste good and evil for themselves, and so lost their innocent trust in the Lord God to give them every good thing and protect them from all evil. Then, because their state of mind and heart was no longer in accord with their surroundings, they had to leave the garden.

Milton depicted the departure of Adam and Eve from the Garden of Eden at the end of his great poem *Paradise Lost* in these lines:

> In either hand the hastening angel caught
> Our lingering parents, and to th' eastern gate
> Led them direct, and down the cliff as fast
> To the subjected plain; then disappeared.
> They, looking back, all th' eastern side beheld
> Of Paradise, so late their happy seat, . . .
> Some natural tears they dropped, but wiped them soon;
> The world was all before them, where to choose
> Their place of rest, and Providence their guide.
> They hand in hand, with wandering steps and slow,
> Through Eden took their solitary way.

BOOK XIII, LINES 637-649

"And here *we* are!" said my graduate professor of English literature as he concluded his reading of the great Christian epic. I've always savored the immediacy of the teacher's statement. It sets me firmly in the contemporary predicament, and yet links me with the allegory of a past, golden age. For I believe that this is not just the story of one man and one woman; it is the story of each of us. And, of course, whatever is in our past, on whatever plane of reality— whether sensual, imaginative, or spiritual—is part of our present and indicates our future. So, here we are. The world lies all before us, but where are we going?

The American transcendentalist Amos Bronson Alcott wrote, "Who loves a garden, still his Eden keeps." This sentiment implies that the author didn't think that we need to go anywhere. Our hope is in retaining an innocent love of nature. Alcott (the father of four daughters, among them Louisa May, who wrote *Little Women* and so saved the family fortunes) was an unsuccessful visionary with many lofty ideas of a benign way of educating children that didn't translate well into the harsh pedagogical practices of the nineteenth century. After trying to teach in several schools here and there, Alcott came to rest in Concord, Massachusetts. Like those other Concord dwellers, Emerson and Thoreau, he believed in the profound power within nature to lift the human spirit into a higher realm of being. "Speak to the earth and it shall teach thee" (Job 12:8).

In Concord, the Alcotts had a garden and an orchard from which their home—Orchard House—took its name. As the story goes, Alcott would pick a basket of apples and carry them to his rustic seat beside the road into town. Here he would try to entice passersby to come and discuss philosophy with him by offering them some apples. Nathaniel Hawthorne, whose house was down the road from the Alcotts, used to cut into Concord through the woods, thus avoiding his garrulous neighbor almost as if he were the serpent in the Garden of Eden.

Hawthorne was rather a recluse, and Alcott could be tedious, but I would like to accept the apple and ponder Alcott's statement as a question. In loving my garden, do I still my Eden keep? Yes, in that the love of gardens is a good love if it brings us closer to the eternal Gardener and raises our perception of how spiritual concepts, like natural plants, can blossom and fruit. But no, if we try to claim as our own something that is not ours. Eden isn't ours to keep. It is only a promise of a spiritual state of peace to which we may aspire if we make a new garden of our lives, sow and reap, and bring the labor of our hands back to the creator God.

I remember my childhood home as being Eden-like. I grew up in a delicious paradise of fruit trees of every kind. In spring the trees were a garden of blossoms; in summer and autumn the fruits ripened each in its appointed time and were harvested; in winter the bare branches, interlaced against the evening sunset, held close the dormant buds of next year's crop. Our household moved with the rhythm and flow of the weather and the seasons. My father tended the orchard; my mother was his helpmeet. And I, as a little girl, ran barefoot through the long grass in the lanes between the rows of trees and made garlands of the wildflowers. As a child, I knew that although my daddy put the roots of the saplings in the ground, it was the Lord who made the trees grow.

Trees grow and children grow, and we move away from innocence and sometimes away from the faith of our fathers. Most mature people don't want to go back to childhood, however paradisal it was. Unless we are very naïve, we can't keep our place in Eden once we taste the knowledge of the world's ways of good and evil for ourselves, which adults inevitably do. It appears that an angel puts us out of the garden, but the truth is we need to work for our daily bread, like Adam did, before we can come to paradise.

Blaise Pascal, seventeenth-century French scientist and religious philosopher, wrote, "Man was lost and saved in a garden." As a Christian, Pascal had no doubt that the Garden of Eden was where humankind was lost. And that our salvation is to be found in a garden does not at all surprise any devout gardener, for intuitively we know the parallel between natural and spiritual gardens. But in what garden do we find salvation? Did Pascal think it likely that we would ever wend our way back to the original Garden of Eden? Did he refer, perhaps, to the Garden of Gethsemane? Temptation and prayer are surely part of the process. But I think, more likely, Pascal meant that humankind is saved by the miracle of Easter morning, which also took place in a garden.

> Now in the place where He was crucified there was a garden, and in the garden a new tomb in which no one had yet been laid. So there they laid Jesus.
>
> **JOHN 19:41-42**

[Mary] turned around and saw Jesus standing there, and did not know that it was Jesus. Jesus said to her, "Woman why are

you weeping? Whom are you seeking?" She, supposing Him to
be the gardener, said to Him, "Sir, if You have carried Him
away, tell me where You have laid Him, and I will take Him
away." Jesus said to her, "Mary!" She turned and said to Him,
"Rabboni!" (which is to say, Teacher). . . . Mary Magdalene
came and told the disciples that she had seen the Lord.

JOHN 20:14-16, 18

That Mary Magdalene should suppose Jesus to be the gardener
wasn't just a case of mistaken identity. He is the gardener of the
whole wide created world, and of our individual minds and hearts,
also. But the recognition that the risen Christ was her living Lord
came only when she called him "Rabboni," or teacher. He is the
only one who can teach the true knowledge of what is good and
what is evil. To live by this knowledge is to be saved. So, we bring
flowers to church on Easter morning to recreate on the chancel a
floral setting where Christ can symbolically rise again to restore the
tree of life.

In the middle of its street, and on either side of the river, was
the tree of life, which bore twelve fruits, each tree yielding its
fruit every month. The leaves of the tree were for the healing
of the nations.

REVELATION 22:2

This miraculous tree planted by the river in the holy city, new
Jerusalem, was to form a new kind of garden in the heavens and in
the Christian church. What Emanuel Swedenborg said about the
place of heavenly gardens in our spiritual lives will be taken up in a
later chapter.

Another eighteenth-century writer considering the way to the
life of goodness was the French philosopher Voltaire. At the end of
his novel *Candide,* the author brings home his hero, abused by men
and battered by terrible misfortune. Candide and two of his
world-weary traveling companions encounter an old man sitting in
peace outside his door. When asked if he had a great estate, the old
man replied, "I have only twenty acres. I cultivate them with my

children; and work keeps at bay three great evils: boredom, vice, and need." In reflecting on the contented and useful life of the old man and his family, Candide determines that the answer to adversity is to follow this example and cultivate his garden. Pangloss, ever the philosopher, expounds that without all the evils and misfortunes Candide has passed through, he could not be where he is.

"'Tis well said," replied Candide, "but we must cultivate our gardens."

This may seem like an unusual sentiment to be expressed in a book written by a learned and sophisticated man of the Enlightenment, and indeed Voltaire suppressed the novel for twelve years for fear it would harm his reputation. We may feel it is even further from a philosophy that suits the end of the twentieth century. But in his recent book, *Drawing Life*, David Gelernter makes reference to Candide's words in this statement: "I'm not sure whether each man cultivating his garden is not our only shot at saving the world." The author, an academic and a computer scientist, was the innocent recipient of a letter bomb. Maimed though he was by the insidious attack, I don't think that Gelernter is bitterly advocating isolation from a wicked world, but rather that the world will only be saved when each one of us, with God's help, makes of our self a better person.

> And Lot lifted his eyes and saw all the plain of Jordan, that it
> was well watered everywhere . . . like the garden of the Lord.
>
> **GENESIS 13:10**

In this biblical story, Abraham and Lot are at the parting of the ways, and Lot has to make a choice which way to go. The beautiful land seems to stretch before him, full of opportunities for a prosperous and peaceful life. So he chooses the plain, the place of lush pastures, and settles there. But he pitches his tent toward Sodom. For him, the vision of the garden of the Lord has evaporated like a mirage in the desert.

Unfortunately, like Lot, we often seem to find ourselves not in paradise, as we expected, but dwelling in one of the cities of the plain, in a Sodom or Gomorrah, both spiritually and physically. All around is a land of smog, acid rain, and filthy trash, as Gerard Manley Hopkins so horribly describes in his poem "God's Grandeur":

> All is seared with trade; bleared, smeared with toil;
> And wears man's smudge and shares man's smell.

How do we save the earth and ourselves from the mire? Environmental endeavors don't seem to have made much difference in cleaning up the world; every day the news has stories of toxic wastes seeping into the earth and the rivers. Humankind isn't doing any better in cleaning up the crime and cruelty that blights society.

In his sonnet, the poet suggests that God is the salvation of the tarnished world. He writes:

> And for all this, nature is never spent;
> There lives the dearest freshness deep down things.

Despite the way we trash the earth, the natural garden does thrive wherever God plants it. His "nature is never spent," for our environment is freshly created every spring out of drab, dead winter. The waste lot behind the supermarket becomes an impressionist painting; drifts of white, lavender-pink, and yellow flowers catch the sunlight. Along the littered roadsides, in season, grow star-of-Bethlehem, blue chicory, yellow bird's-foot trefoil, toadflax, and Queen Anne's lace. Even the black and tarry macadam can't keep down the dandelion, which thrusts green clawlike leaves and a yellow mane up through the crack and crumble at the highway's edge. In nature, God creates anew the beauty of the earth, and in our souls the same.

Nature is in a constant process of renewing and unfolding the inspiration and truth of its Creator. But it is not enough to read only in the book of nature, so we turn to the Word of God, or the Bible. Several years ago, I began to wonder just how many times growing things and gardens are used in the Word to depict the nature of the human spirit. For interest's sake, I decided to note these Bible references as I found them while reading. Genesis has many, with the creation of the Earth and the planting of the garden eastward in Eden. This pastoral emphasis continues, though gardens are not mentioned as specifically after those early chapters. In the back of my 1994–1995 journal (the one I was keeping at the time I became interested in searching out these references), I compiled a list of more than forty scriptural passages about growing things, which I found in a rather quick scanning of the Old Testament. (A friend who tried this on a computer search found 1,527 references in the whole Bible to gardens and fields, their cultivation, trees, herbs, grapevines, and so on.)

Here are a very few of the many inspiring passages from the Old Testament that I love:

> And the earth brought forth grass, the herb that yields seed according to its kind, and the tree that yields fruit, whose seed is in itself according to its kind. And God saw that it was good.
>
> **GENESIS 1:12**

> The Lord will comfort Zion,
> He will comfort all her waste places;
> He will make her wilderness like Eden,
> And her desert like the garden of the Lord;
> Joy and gladness will be found in it,
> Thanksgiving and the voice of melody.
>
> **ISAIAH 51:3**

> Thus says the Lord God:
> You were the seal of perfection,
> Full of wisdom and perfect in beauty.
> You were in Eden, the garden of God.
>
> **EZEKIEL 28:12-13**

Gardens in the Bible are often associated with water: rivers and rain, dewdrops and fountains. Of course, water is essential for the growth of vegetation, and so truth for the flowering of the human mind. A dry and unproductive land is like a parched mind and a barren heart; it brings forth no fruit worth the eating, no beauty to delight. The person who flourishes will be planted like a tree by the river. He or she will blossom as the rose in the desert under spring rain. Promises of natural abundance reflect the spiritual abundance given by the Lord as a blessing for the upright, the diligent gardeners, the faithful shepherds.

> How lovely are your tents, O Jacob!
> Your dwellings, O Israel!
> Like valleys that stretch out,
> Like gardens by the riverside.
> Like aloes planted by the Lord,
> Like cedars beside the waters.
>
> **NUMBERS 24:5-6**

> Blessed of the Lord is his land,
> With the precious things of heaven, with the dew
> And the deep lying beneath,
> With the precious fruits of the sun,
> With the precious produce of the months. . . .
>
> **DEUTERONOMY 33:13-14**

> He shall be like a tree
> Planted by the rivers of water,
> That brings forth its fruit in its season,
> Whose leaf also shall not wither;
> And whatever he does shall prosper.
>
> **PSALM 1:3**

> You shall be embarrassed because of the gardens
> Which you have chosen.
> For you shall be as a terebinth whose leaf fades,
> And as a garden that has no water.
>
> **ISAIAH 1:29-30**

The New Testament has many pastoral references, also. Jesus speaks of seeds, wheat and tares, fig trees, and vineyards in the parables particularly. His message about the kingdom of heaven and the kind of life we must want to live in order to be dwellers in the kingdom is given in figurative language and metaphor.

I like to believe that my wildflower garden is a metaphor for my life. The garden didn't start out with such high symbolic purpose, and it certainly isn't one that I think of every time that I work or wander there. But the older I grow (and I hope I am growing like a flower, not a weed), the more I see connections that have eternal ends. I see the cycles of winter and spring, death and rebirth enacted every year in my physical garden here in southeastern Pennsylvania, and also in the garden of my being. Sometimes I am in a moribund state, and sometimes I feel a rebirth of spiritual hope as full of promise as a spring day.

1987

MARCH 29

Today I took an early Sunday morning walk. By 9:00 A.M., I was back and standing among the daffodils and celandine in my wildflower garden when the bells from the white church on the hill above the town of Huntingdon Valley began to chime. I thought of Emily Dickinson, her poem about going to church in a garden, and also of that more sentimental verse by Dorothy Gurney, which nevertheless reflects some of my own feeling:

> *The kiss of the sun for pardon*
> *The song of the birds for mirth—*
> *One is nearer God's heart in a garden*
> *Than anywhere else on earth.*

Returning for a moment to Candide and David Gelernter and their admonition that we should cultivate our gardens, we might ponder on how cultivating our garden makes us a better person. How does it bring us closer to God and in harmony with other people, and in touch with our spirit? Here are some more notes from my journals that suggest connections between my natural garden and the one I'm trying to cultivate in my mind and heart:

1989

JULY 1

A new month. A chance to make a new beginning. I'm always grateful that the Lord has arranged our time and space—moons, seasons, places—so that we have many chances to make fresh starts in our lives. The month of June was a stressful time for our family. But as we sat at peace in the garden last evening, we talked about the way things do work out if we don't worry about them too much and trust in the Lord.

> *Seedtime and harvest,*
> *Cold and heat,*
> *Winter and summer,*
> *And day and night . . . .*

GENESIS 8:22

As much as we try to manipulate events, they happen in the Lord's time.

1990

FEBRUARY 19

Lovely afternoon—windy, but 57° in the sun. The first periwinkle is blooming at the base of the Norway maple by the path. How we delight in each new promise of the renewal of the earth, the renewal of our souls.

JULY 1

We had just started out for a walk after supper in the strange amber light, under a skyful of pink, gray, and white clouds, when it began to rain. We saw a neighbor at the end of the street, standing in his garden. He pointed out a rainbow in the east—Noah's sign. We stood in companionable silence under his tree to look at it with him.

1991

FEBRUARY 21

My goodness, what a dazzling day! My goodness, everyone's goodness— our light of truth and warmth of love—comes from the heavenly sun. With this radiance within it, no wonder the earthly sun makes us feel so alive and happy.

JULY 9

The plumes of the purple buddleia under our bedroom window are open-ing, and just in the nick of time. Saw a beautiful yellow swallowtail but-terfly today—the first. It is part of God's plan, and not a coincidence, that the butterfly bush is ready for the butterfly.

1992

FEBRUARY 2

Groundhog Day. Sun makes shadow, and we assume that the groundhog that lives under our old burn pile behind the garden shed saw his and was frightened back into his burrow for six more weeks of winter. The day is cold and windy, as well as sunny, so we can believe the prediction. In six weeks, will Mother still be lying dormant in the winter-white bed of the nursing home or will the Lord have called her to a spiritual spring-time of awakening and rebirth? "God only knows." Like the groundhog, we aren't the predictors; we only cast the shadows.

1993

DECEMBER 27

Seventeen degrees above zero at 8:00 A.M. Frosted ferns on the window-panes, as intricate in frond as those that grow in the wild garden in the summer, demonstrate the connatus of all things to a higher plane of life. The humblest things of nature hold the secrets of the universe and its creator.

1994

NOVEMBER 28

At the end of November, spring seems very far away. I console myself with the thought that creation is not static. It is organic and going on all the time. Lower forms aspire to higher forms with a freedom to evolve, as frost crystals make fern fronds, or a rose becomes an apple tree.

And the process of creation is going on all the time in human minds, too. Because we are spiritual beings, we are given even greater freedom to change, to grow upward and evolve, as it were, into a higher being with a

better will to do good for the neighbor and love the Lord, and a more per-
fect understanding of how to do it. We grow in the heat and light of the
spiritual sun, or we die at heart. The difference between life and death is
purpose—not health, or chance, or natural talent—but how we fulfill
God's purpose for us. His purpose is always for us to become the higher
form, the higher use. There is the connatus we feel to make ourselves into a
new form, and then the new form itself that he creates in us—process and
product. My life in process is, I hope, becoming like a garden of the Lord.

It was an old-fashioned gardener of my mother's generation
who first mentioned "the Lord's garden" not as a far-off place in the
Bible or a theoretical idea, but in connection with a particular spot
on her property. She and I were having a conversation years ago
about gardening. "I have two gardens that really keep me busy," she
said, "a vegetable garden and a flower garden. Both have the usual
weeds and pests, natural evils that I work very hard to keep under
control, as I work to subdue my sins. But across the driveway, under
a big tree, is another garden, full of wildflowers. There everything
thrives. I call it the Lord's garden."

The sun, breaking through the lingering clouds,
sets every raindrop sparkling and touches
the Dutchman's-breeches hung out on the line to dry.

An Early Spring

SPRING IS IN THE MIND LONG BEFORE
IT IS IN THE GARDEN.

I was relieved to hear the weatherman from the Schyulkill Valley Nature Center, say one morning several years ago (before the WFLN radio station became defunct), that meteorological winter is from December 1 to March 1. Reckoning by the equinox for the beginning of fall and spring never made any sense to me. Every gardener is aware that winter has well begun around here by early in the month of December, because most vegetation has stopped to rest for a while. Even the plants and shrubs that stay green are on hold. And we know in our bones that spring starts stirring weeks before March 20 or 21, especially in the years when there has been a mild winter. There is no precise and official start to spring. How could anyone presume to say, "Spring came in this morning at 6:42," as if nature ran by a stopwatch?

The old adage is that March comes in like a lion and goes out like a lamb, but sometimes the weather does a reverse, comes in gentle and then roars out, or rampages at both ends and curls up like a pussycat in the warm sun in the middle. In my March journals, the recording of sunny warm days and dismal cold ones alternates. Experience teaches that spring is a seesaw. There can be uncannily hot days dragging summerlike thunderstorms up out of the west, or cold winds that toss the branches and whip the buds around and batter the daffodils. Even if we haven't gotten a flake of snow all winter, there always seems to be snow in late March. "The onion snow," my mother used to call it.

Spring is suspense. When I was growing up on the old farm, the earliest signs of spring for me were the speckled purple bloom of the skunk cabbage in the swamp and the pulsating evening chorus of the tiny frogs called spring peepers. I rarely hear them where I live now. Sometimes their piping calls come up from the damp woods at the bottom of the road, but the air currents have to be just right, and I have to be outside, listening hard. Instead, like most of the people on spring watch, I tritely anticipate the first robin to put the seal on spring's arrival.

Robins have usually made their appearance in flocks by the second week of March, but often they come earlier. After I had seen some robins scratching in the snow around the feeder in February one year, I asked one of our local birders about it. Is it a case of survival of the fittest? Robins becoming seed eaters when the worms are frozen up tight underground? He told me that he thinks some are even wintering over now, retreating into the thick woods in the coldest weather.

> The north wind doth blow, and we shall have snow.
> And what shall poor Robin do then? Poor thing!

1988

MARCH 9

Just after talking about how it was time to see the first robin, we saw one out of the kitchen window, scratching away by the hedge and then hopping over the lawn in a proprietary fashion. I'm sure the same robins come back every year and feel that they own the place. Tomorrow there may be sleek robins in brown suits and ruddy vests parading all over the lawn.

Last night, Bruce was reading to me about the blizzard of 1888 from Yankee Magazine. *The blizzard—seventy-mile-an-hour winds, blinding snow, and bitter cold—came in March after a spell of mild weather just like we've been having. Although I've never seen anything that fierce, we do frequently get our heaviest snowfalls in March. So, however warm the days, it is foolish to take the leaf cover off the gardens, and vain to count the robin as a sure sign of spring. But we do it anyway.*

1990

MARCH 25

Snow in the night. Courageous daffodils have bent to adversity and risen again, but the eyes of the celandine are shut up tight.

That last journal entry reminded me of Shakespeare's lines from *A Winter's Tale*:

> Daffodils that come before the swallow dares
> And take the winds of March with Beauty.

There is another poem about daffodils by the English romantic poet William Wordsworth:

> . . . I saw a crowd,
> A host of golden daffodils;
> Beside the lake, beneath the trees,
> Fluttering and dancing in the breeze.

My garden dream was to have a Wordsworthian "crowd, a host of golden daffodils" filling the spaces under the trees with their own yellow sunshine as the winter white of snowdrops melted away. But early on, my bulbs didn't seem to be naturalizing very fast, so I asked Phyllis, my daughter's teacher, if I could dig a few more from her woods. She told me to help myself. "The bulbs need separating anyway," she said. "Everything grows abundantly out there in the woods. The earth's as rich as fruitcake." The soil in my garden is not so rich as the dark, moist groom's cake of Phyllis's native Canada, but in later years, my daffodils have been proliferating too, and I do have gallant patches of them now. It is a joy to go out and gather them without fear of denuding the garden.

1992

MARCH 28

Today, I picked a handful of daffodils from around the yard and in the wild garden. They look cheerful here in the bedroom and bring the spring indoors to Bruce, who is no longer able to go out to meet it.

I have a variety of DAFFODILS, some rather exotic with pale petals and ruffled orange or pink trumpets, whose names escape me unless I look them up in a bulb catalog. I am confused, too, about the differences between daffodils, jonquils, and narcissus. Mother gave me bulbs of what she called white narcissus: two kinds, Poetica, with a flat red-and-yellow trumpet, and Thalia, with two pale flowers on one stem. I love them because they remind me of my mother and her garden. But there is one daffodil that is a pure yellow, the trumpet just a shade darker than the petals. I like to think that this is similar to the one growing naturally in the haunts of Wordsworth in the English Lake District.

1993

APRIL 18

In this first spring since Bruce's physical death, the golden trumpets of the daffodils proclaim for me the promise of the Lord Jesus Christ's words, "I am the resurrection and the life." They are such strong, simple flowers, deep and glowing, with a fresh scent like the earth after rain.

In remembrance of one of our spring anniversaries, Bruce once gave me a copy of *Leaves from Gerard's Herball*, arranged for garden lovers by Marcus Woodward. The paperback edition reproduces much of the original text of the 1597 version and many of the woodcuts. John Gerard describes the daffodil:

> The common wilde Daffodil groweth wilde in fields and sides of woods in the West parts of England. . . . It hath long fat and thick leaves, full of slimie juice; among which riseth up a bare thicke stalke, hollow within and full of juice. The floure groweth at the top, of a yellowish white colour, with a yellow

crown or circle in the middle, and floureth in the moneth of
Aprill and sometimes sooner. The root is of a bulbous fashion.

As well as descriptions of the plants, Gerard includes their med-
icinal uses. This was one of the prime reasons flower gardens were
maintained in Medieval and Renaissance times. By scientific stan-
dards, these home remedies are considered obsolete, but I find
them historically fascinating. And it is interesting that here, in the
end of the twentieth century, there is a revival of herbal healing.

> Galen [of Greek parentage, court physician to Marcus
> Aurelius, was the medical authority for the late Middle Ages
> and Renaissance] saith, that the roots of Narcissus have such
> wonderful qualities in drying, that they consound and glew
> together very great wounds, yea and such gashes or cuts as
> happen about the veins, sinues, and tendons. They have also a
> certaine clensing facultie.
>
> The root of Narcissus stamped with hony and applied
> plaister-wise, helpeth them that are burned with fire. . . . The
> same applied with hony and nettle seed helpeth Sun burning.
> Being stamped with meale of Darnel and hony, it draweth
> forth thorns and stubs out of any part of the body.

Gerard was a man of wide classical learning, and as well as the
words of Galen, the physician, he recounts portions of Theocritus,
who wrote verses about daffodils. It was when Lady Europa and her
maidens came to gather these flowers in the Greek meadows, he
tells us, that they encountered Zeus in the form of a bull who carried off the lady and ravished her. This myth recalls to my mind another about the beautiful youth Narcissus who, stooping to drink at
a woodland pool, saw his reflection in the still water and fell in love
with it. Where he sat and pined away, a lovely flower grew to which
his name was given: Narcissus.

My spring garden itself is like an illustrated book. Almost every
plant has some association with healing or legend, story or song.

Flowers do seem to inspire poetry. For instance, in looking through a copy of Wordsworth's selected poems just now, in search of the exact words of his famous verse about daffodils, I found another flower poem, titled "To The Small Celandine." Neither this poem nor the flower is as well-known as "Daffodils" (although knowledge of "Celandine" is spreading with the plant).

> Ere a leaf is on a bush,
> In the time before the thrush
> Has a thought about her nest,
> Thou wilt come with half a call,
> Spreading out thy glossy breast
> Like a careless Prodigal;
> Telling tales about the sun,
> When we've little warmth, or none.
> Spring is coming, Thou art come.

I'm amused by Mr. Wordsworth; although he pledges his love for the little flower and praises where no other poet does (he tells us), he is surely on to its spreading characteristics, for in the second verse he goes on:

> Careless of thy neighbourhood,
> Thou dost show thy pleasant face
> On the moor, and in the wood,
> In the lane;—there's not a place,
> Howsoever mean it be,
> But 't is good enough for thee.

1985

MARCH 14

There are tints of color in the trees, a pale imitation of autumn reds and golds. We spent a happy afternoon with two of our grandchildren in Tyler Park. Along the creek there were bright clumps of celandine already blooming. When I was a child and played so much in the woods, there wasn't a trace of it. Now this starry-eyed flower seems to be all over. It is like the spring tide, for it flows like green water with a froth of yellow,

reaching the farthest nooks and crannies of the garden. It seeps every-
where, even through the privet hedge and out onto the lawn.

1991

MARCH 28

Today the lawn got its first mowing of the season, mostly to chop off the
wild garlic. There isn't much height to the grass yet, but weeds are up, and
wildflowers. Bruce left a tuft of bright yellow celandine on the back lawn,
which made me think of Frost's poem "Tuft of Flowers," although that
was a much taller flower.

As I stand here in my wildflower garden in the March sun, with
the buds of the low-growing lesser celandine just opening around
me, I am reminded of how it all began and the family trip we took to
Fromuth's Nursery to purchase the first plants for the garden.

The Fromuth house and garden business was in Holland,
Pennsylvania, a small hamlet on the Neshaminy Creek about five
miles north of Bryn Athyn. I always loved coming round the bend of
the road and through the tunnel under the train track to see, across
a farmer's field, the little yellow house perched on the steep bank,
with a glass greenhouse beside it and makeshift cold frames ter-
raced up the hillside. Just by their house, the road runs on over a
bridge crossing the dam by an old grist mill. Many years ago, when
water-powered machinery became obsolete, other uses were found
for the stone building, and afterwards it was converted into the Mill
Race Inn. The gears and grindstones are still preserved inside the
inn as a curiosity for the diners.

On the day we came to buy wildflowers at Fromuth's, it was very
warm and the greenhouse door was ajar; the glass covers of the cold
frames were tilted up or askew lest the growing plants burn under the
direct rays of the sun. We parked our car on the level graveled space
off the road and got out. Our two children raced like kid goats up the
steep bank to where a kneeling figure was setting out young plants in
rows in the brown soil. Bruce and I followed at a slower climb.

"If you want to buy something," Mr. Fromuth called down to us, "get the Missus. She's in the house."

In answer to our knock on the blue door, Mrs. Fromuth came out, a cheerful, bent little woman with a flowered cotton bib apron over her housedress.

"You want some wildflowers? Well, I'll show you what we have left," she said, leading us along one of the narrow paths between the cold frames. "It's late, though, and most of the spring plants are gone."

Along the path was a creeping plant with fuzzy, scalloped gray-green leaves, flowering with lavender-pink heads. It bordered the path and pushed up against the weathered wood of the cold frames. It was pretty. I asked what it was; my knowledge of wildflowers was just budding. I now know it as hairy or downy wood mint. But Mrs. Fromuth didn't give it a name. She said, "Oh, that's just a weed. Grows everywhere. You don't want that in your garden." She shook her wispy gray head, then smiled at my daughter, Rachel, who was bending over to pick a handful of the blooms. "But take all you want." With that Thane, boylike, pulled up a clump—roots and all—to take home, where it is still alive and well and living in the garden.

We took most of the well-known wildflowers that Mrs. Fromuth had left: pale pink hepaticas, primroses, several mertensia or Virginia bluebells, one or two Dutchman's-breeches, a frail-looking rue anemone. Then from another frame, we chose two plants of lesser celandine, which I'd never seen or heard of before. With sun-bright yellow flowers, it was appealing, and I was tempted to take more.

"They'll spread, you know," Mrs. Fromuth said. How right she was.

LESSER CELANDINE (*Ranunculus ficaria*): The authors of American wildflower books don't seem to think much of this small plant; some ignore it altogether. Peterson gives it three lines and a black-and-white drawing in *A Field Guide to Wildflowers*, labeling it an *alien*. Perhaps that accounts for the snobbery toward this humble but very prolific foreigner.

But Stokoe, in his book of British wildflowers, treats this member of the buttercup family more kindly, more in the way of Wordsworth:

> The burnished gold stars of this charming little plant will be found as early as February on sunny banks and below pasture hedges or by the roadside. The bright golden flower consists of the sepals varying from three to five, usually three, and the petals numbering from seven to twelve.
>
> Its roots produce a large number of cylindrical tubers, each of which is capable of producing a new plant, and reproduction is thus speedily effected.
>
> PAGE 23

I omitted the description of the leaves from the Stokoe entry because they differ from the ones I see on my celandine, which are like those in Peterson's drawing. But I attribute this to variation caused by the flower having traveled across the Atlantic and adapted to new conditions. Peterson, in his introduction to *A Field Guide to Wildflowers*, says that this variation often happens even as a plant moves around from one location to another in the same general area. The rest of the identification is the same, although in my garden the leaves may appear in February; the bright stars don't start to burst open before mid-March—and then only one by one in the sunniest spots.

It wasn't until I looked up the lesser celandine in the field guides that I realized it is in the buttercup family. The bright green leaves reminded me of the watercress that grew around the springhouse below my old home, so I assumed it was in the cress family, but I was wrong. Two of the other plants that we chose at Fromuth's are also in this prolific Ranunculaceae family: the hepatica and the rue anemone.

The HEPATICA (*Hepatica americana*) comes in early spring and is native to the eastern half of the United States and adjacent Canada. First come the hairy reddish-brown stems with the flower bud tucked into bracts of the same color, then the leaves emerge, and the flowers open. But one has to look closely to see the hepaticas even when they are blooming. The flowers are shy and small, about a half-inch across, with six to ten pale pink, lavender, or white petals, which Peterson tells me are really sepals. They only rise about four or five inches from a group of basal leaves with rounded lobes. There is a related hepatica with pointed leaves (*acutiloba*) and showier flowers. I think we may have had one of those and two of the round-lobed ones. Unfortunately, today I have none. I moved them once too often to escape the rising tide of celandine, and tired of having me try to run their lives, they gave up. It is one of the wild-flowers that I would like to reestablish in the garden.

RUE ANEMONE (*Anemonella thalictroides*) is so named, I suppose, because the appearance of the whorl of leaves (or bracts) on the slender stem is similar to those of the herb called rue. The real leaves are basal, but look similar, much divided and with saw-toothed edges. The rue anemone is one of my favorites; it is a flower that I watch for eagerly, as usually it does not bloom until mid-April. The small, open-faced, fairylike flower is white or faintly pink. The whole plant has a delicate air and appeals to my sense of protection for the small and meek against the strong and tough. But I suspect it is more hardy than it appears because it has taken hold and even spread in a modest way. Several years ago, when the whole garden was suffering from human and canine encroachment and I thought I might have to abandon it, I moved some of the rue anemones to a shady spot in another part of my yard. They took up residence there without demure. So my experience would agree with Edgar T. Wherry, in his *Wild Flower Guide*, that they are "readily cultivated in a woodland garden."

MERTENSIA or VIRGINIA BLUEBELL (*Mertensia virginica*), one of my husband's favorites, is a member of the Borage family and related to the rough-leafed borage that grows in the herb garden. These leaves are oval, smooth, and strongly veined. The stem is also smooth and succulent. The leaves start up out of the ground—a purple-green color—in March, but the plant does not reach its height of two feet or more and bloom until April, unless the days have been unusually warm. The nodding, trumpet-like blue flowers are pink in bud, and the pink and blue together in the cluster gives something of the color tones of a Renoir painting. When the plant is finished blooming in May, the whole thing withers away to nothing in a week or two.

The spring that we were courting, Bruce drove round and round the back roads of Bucks County, Pennsylvania, near the Neshaminy Creek looking for a particular patch of pink-and-blue Mertensia to show me. He remembered being taken by an older couple (adopted grandparents of the children of his first family) to visit a spot where a whole bank of mertensia was blooming along the roadside. But we never found it, not that spring nor the next. Perhaps we found the right place, but the flowers were over. Or perhaps it was an experience from another phase of his life that we were not meant to repeat. We were fortunate to have them flourish later in our own wild garden, only a lawn away from our kitchen door.

The primroses we brought from Fromuth's were more like the ones you can buy in supermarkets or florist shops, which will grow if you plant them out in our eastern gardens, and not like those native American ones described in either Wherry or Peterson. For a description of the PRIMROSE (*Primula vulgaris*), we have to return again to England and Stokoe's British guidebook.

> [This] is a perennial with thick, fleshy root stock underground, from which spring the tuft of soft, wrinkled leaves and the crowd of flower-buds at their heart. The underside of the leaf is covered by a network of stout veins and is softly hairy.

> The flowers are on long, slender footstalks of a pinkish colour, all springing from one common stout flower-stem, which is so short as to be hidden among the bases of the leaves. The flowers [are] . . . about one and a half inches across, and of a very delicate tint of pale greenish-yellow; the mouth of the tube encircled by five triangular patches of deeper yellow. The great flowering time is during April and May.

PAGE 166

55

The soft yellow coloring that Stokoe mentions here refers to primroses in a natural state. The ones we see most often for sale are in really vibrant shades of gold, red, and purple-blue. And although they are pretty in the house, pastel yellow is the shade that I much prefer in the wild garden. The Fromuths only had two plants left the day that we were there, so we took them both, one yellow, one magenta. Wouldn't you know, it would be the garish one that survived and multiplied?

Gerard has the primrose in his herbal and says that "some one or other of them do floure all Winterlong." He calls them *Primula veris*, "because they floure with the first." I have found this to be true of some yellow primroses (a recent acquisition) I planted beside the birdbath. I admire them from the dining-room window, budding and flowering in the most unlikely times. Perhaps this year, I'll try moving some of them back into the wildflower garden. Gerard mentions that primroses were boiled up with rose and betony water, sugar, salt, pepper, and butter, strained, and used as a spring tonic to cure the "phrensie," by a certain London practitioner of Gerard's time. Even without all the added ingredients, just the sight of primroses is a tonic for this gardener's spring fever.

Another purchase we made at Mrs. Fromuth was of two lacy-leafed little plants, quaintly called DUTCHMAN'S-BREECHES. I wonder if the flower might have been first discovered and named in and around the Dutch colony of New Amsterdam, because the individual flowerets on the pinkish stem do resemble Dutch burghers' pantaloons turned upside down, ankles to the sky. One of the original plants still survives in my garden, tucked under the spirea bush by the maple stump. Its breeches are vaguely pink. The ones I have seen growing in the wild are white with a suggestion of yellow.

This flower is a member of the widespread and prolific poppy clan, in the bleeding heart subfamily, *Dicentra cucullaria*. The delicate leaves are much dissected and gray-green like the wild bleeding heart, and the shape of the flowers is not dissimilar.

I can still see Mrs. Fromuth's thick-knuckled, wrinkled hands as she gently troweled the plants we wanted from the rich soil and wrapped them in sheets of newspaper. While she went into the house to get our change, her husband came stumping down the hill in his high-topped, earth-encrusted shoes, heavy rubber pads strapped for protection around his knees. "Thought I recognized you," he said to my husband. They exchanged talk about former days when Harry Fromuth used to be the head gardener at an estate on the outskirts of Bryn Athyn that Bruce visited sometimes. Mrs. Fromuth came back, and we stood chatting in the beneficent noontime until the restless children made it evident it was time to say goodbye. Each child was allowed to carry a parcel carefully to the car, where they argued, of course, about who got to sit where.

Like sun on my shoulders, I feel the warm blessing of two dear old people who had led a life loving and caring for growing things together. Their blessing came with the flowers we bought that day, and lingers still in my garden. And from those two small celandine plants wrapped in newspaper has come all this tide of bright green that engulfs the garden today and says, *spring* more clearly than any date on the calendar.

Before we had the wildflower garden, we used to go more frequently to the famous Longwood Gardens on the border of Pennsylvania and Delaware, over an hour's drive away. January and February could be endured, but when the calendar page turned to March, we felt we couldn't wait any longer for some color in our drab lives. It was best to go on a cold, bleak day, one with a few snow flurries, if possible. Then the glory of Easter lilies and bright tulips, and the stretches of amazingly green grass inside the big conservatories, would burst over us with the excitement of fireworks. Every year, the gardeners there had a different display of beauty to delight our senses. But it wasn't variety that we craved; it was assurance that spring would come. For two or three hours we wandered the walkways, the smell of warm, moist earth and flowers transporting us to a better world, as if we'd died and gone to heaven.

When enough spring had soaked in to last for a week or two, we got back in the car and drove home to winter.

Another favorite excursion to take in March was the trip into town by train to the annual Philadelphia Flower Show:

1987

MARCH 12

Today was a perfect day to go to the flower show—raw and damp outside, a burst of spring inside. The exhibits were all wonderful, fresh and inspiring. Vicks Wild Garden, as always, spurs me to new attempts in my own amateur garden. There was another woodsy garden that we especially liked planted informally on a hillside with azaleas, rhododendrons, grape hyacinth, and daffodils blooming along the little stream that flowed out from under the stone springhouse that we liked especially. It would be nice to have some water in our garden as a focus.

In the category of Storybook Gardens (nostalgic gardens from the past) was a delightful Peter Rabbit Garden, and another called a Child's Garden of Verses. Many of these gardens had plantings of hollyhocks, delphinium, and foxgloves—old-fashioned and charming. I came away with visions of flowers like sugar plums dancing in my head.

The trick, of course, is to sustain the vision long enough to put it into practice. The seed and garden catalogs, with their glossy colored pictures, stream in by mail in the gloom of February days, bringing on dreams of magnificent beds and borders that somehow never do quite become summer reality.

There is something very satisfying about a wildflower garden where the purpose is not show. Although there are catalogs for wildflowers now, the whole enterprise seems less slick, more natural. And the gardener's role is humble, not proprietary, an underlying acknowledgment that this is God's garden. What grows and blooms is always a happy surprise, as if one were there at the genesis of the earth, a witness to the "let there be" of creation.

1986

MARCH 31

In spite of the intense cold of just a week ago, the flowers have pushed through the contrariness of the weather to bloom in time for April. Not snow, nor sleet, nor freezing rain shall stop the postman of spring from his appointed rounds.

Perhaps the state of true spring is like regeneration; it's not the externals of our temperament, but what's going on inside, in the secret heart of the earth, that matters.

1989

MARCH 30

The sultry, summery weather of the Easter weekend has burst the buds on the saucer magnolia and brought eight flowers into bloom in the wild garden. The Dutchman's- breeches sprang up leaf, stem, and buds all in one day. But I don't really like it when all the flowers come in a rush. I love it when spring comes in slowly—then the joy of its arrival is almost painful, each opening blossom like a tiny stab of delight. For every flower holds uncountable treasure and should be savored.

I read in Swedenborg, "There was once opened before the angels a flower as to its interiors which are called spiritual; and when they saw it, they said that there was a whole paradise therein, which consisted of things ineffable" (De Verbo 19:2). Because of the spiritual, we respond in the natural realm with delight.

As March goes out and high spring comes in, I feel joyful to be a small part of it. The garden is my re-creation.

> Once we become interested in the progress of the plants in our care their development becomes a part of the rhythm of our own lives, and we are refreshed.
>
> **THALUSSA CRUSO**

1990

MARCH 31

When I got home at 5:00 P.M. from working in the stuffy library all the rainy afternoon, I went into the wildflower garden. The rain had stopped; everything was drenched and fresh, the garden glowing with white narcissus in green light, the air chilly and still.

I came into the house with bits of sodden leaves clinging to my soaked docksiders, Bruce, who had seen me from the window, asked me what I had been doing out there. I tried to explain that the cold, rain-wet garden was the essence of early spring. He said I was like Thoreau.

1993

MARCH 27

Outside in the chill, wind-driven mist, every sort of call, honk, squawk, trill, peep, churrip, whistle, tweet, drum roll, rasp, and coo is blending in a bird chorus as ancient as spring itself and as up-to-date as this morning.

1996

MARCH 31

This morning, the sun is bright, the air clear and cool. March is gamboling out like a spring lamb no lions for us, unless they are dandelions.

Extending her influence and her love were the flowers
transplanted from my mother's garden to mine—
among them the early pink azalea.

A GARLAND OF GARDENERS

SHOW ME YOUR GARDEN AND I SHALL TELL YOU WHO YOU ARE.
ALFRED AUSTIN

When I'm in the garden, I'm rarely sad or lonely. Each plant has a tale to tell of where it came from, as well as the record of its life since it arrived in my garden. Only a few flowers have crept in without a history, though a lot of weeds have. As each flower comes into blossom and catches my special attention, I remember its story. Some were purchased, like those which came from Fromuth's Nursery, some were gathered on foraging excursions that I'll describe later, but many came from other gardeners. These are the flowers I treasure most, gifts that remind me of the spirit of the people who gave them to me.

This chapter's title, "A Garland of Gardeners," is a play on the fanciful yet politically correct terms of the chase that were actually applied to hunting in fifteenth-century England. James Lipton gathered these together in an amusing and delightful book, called *An Exhalation of Larks*. In the last section, the author includes some more modern and inclusive metaphors that he has recently discovered, coined himself, or been sent by others. Lipton invites his readers to play the game also, and so I have. This chapter is a floral tribute to several gardeners who have introduced me into the vernal mysteries and encouraged me to be a gardener myself.

There are three especially wonderful women gardeners in my garland: my mother, my husband's Aunt Doris, and Phyllis of the snowdrops. All three are now tending their spiritual gardens, but I feel I still have them by my side when I'm working here in my earthly plot. Their continued presence among the flowers they gave me is one of the reasons the wildflower garden is such a happy place.

Mother

1987

MAY 1

The forget-me-nots are everywhere! When I close my eyes at night, after working all afternoon in the wild garden, I see them twinkling like blue stars in the dark behind my eyelids.

How fitting that my dear mother should have given me the FORGET-ME-NOTS. Their bright eyes (though blue, not brown like hers) and energetic growth, their strong roots and down-to-earth hardiness all remind me of her. To look at my large patch in bloom is to see a cloudless spring sky and feel optimistic about God's providence, as she always did. The flowers often open very early, nestled low down in the emerging leaves; then the branching stems, covered with tiny, intensely blue flowers, grow up to meet the light and warmth of the sun. They take their stand from twelve to fourteen inches high and bloom on at least into June. My plant is not listed in the wildflower guidebooks, like the true wild forget-me-not, *Myosotis scorpioides,* although it is obviously in the same family. Because of its blue flowers and blunt, hairy leaves, it reminds me of the herb borage, and I'm sure that it is in the same family. Peterson does say that there are several alien species of the forget-me-not in our area, so perhaps this is one of them.

My mother came from Canada, an alien herself at first, although she later became a naturalized American citizen. Her parents, of German extraction, were farmers and members of the Swedenborgian congregation in the town of Kitchener, Ontario, around the turn of the century. Mother told stories of good times: church socials and outings, good friends, and close family ties, but life on the farm was hard. As a young woman, she said emphatically that she would never marry a farmer. And then, of course, she married my father, who was a farmer of sorts—an orchardist. But as growing things seemed to be in her genes, it would have been a shame to waste her talent on city life. I'm sure that my love of gardening came from my mother, implanted at an early age, long before I was aware that even the work of it could be a pleasure.

Two of my earliest memories of gardens are of the big vegetable garden in back and Mother's flower garden at the side of the farmhouse. In the early spring, there were daffodils and forsythia in this flower garden; later, irises and lilacs; and in the high summer, blue larkspur and little, red field poppies. There was a coarse-leafed, sprawly plant, almost like a squash vine, that bloomed later in August with large, white trumpets; I called them moon flowers because they opened in the evening and attracted the hummingbird moths.

It was this well-established flower garden that I tried to appropriate as my own one year when my girl-scout leader had a best garden contest as incentive to earn the gardening badge. For some reason, I was less than enthusiastic about the project and put off getting started until, suddenly, the summer was half over and the scout leader and two other women gardeners were coming to judge our efforts in a week. I remember begging Mother to help me save face by allowing me to claim part of her garden. With zeal born of procrastination, I labored hard, edging, weeding, even putting in a plant or two. But when the judges came to visit, they did not have the wool pulled over their eyes. Mother didn't give me away, but I suppose it was obvious that this garden wasn't a one-season effort. It was justice, I guess, that another girl won the prize. She had planted zinnia and marigold seeds in straight rows in the corner of the family vegetable garden. Her plants were flourishing, but I thought that, aesthetically, her garden left a lot to be desired. My mother's garden was much prettier, and I had helped, at least a little, to make it so.

During the years of my childhood, my parents and I shared the farmhouse with my father's family. They lived on one side of the house, and we lived on the other. When I was sixteen, my long-widowed grandmother died; my bachelor uncle, who had been living with her, moved out; and we expanded into the whole house. At that time, my mother also expanded her flower gardens, adding one by the path leading to what was now our front door. It was while digging in this garden one day, years after it was planted, that I made a wonderful find.

As a bride, Mother had been beautifully slim, but as the years went by, while she was never obese, her figure definitely became matronly. I used to tell her that it didn't matter whether she was "plump," because there was more to hug. But as she struggled into her girdle and moved into a still-larger dress size, she determined that she was too fat and joined a group of local ladies who were dieting. She did lose quite a lot of weight, and because her fingers got thinner, she also lost her wedding ring. She had no idea where. Distraught, she searched the house; when she couldn't find it anywhere, she begged my father to give her another.

I think that my dad was upset, too, but his response was masculine, rational, and, as it seemed at the time to a romantic teenager, completely hard-hearted. He didn't want to give her a second wedding ring. "Another ring," he said, " wouldn't be the engraved ring I gave you in the wedding ceremony as a symbol of eternal marriage." But then he relented a little and said he'd give her the money to buy one herself, if she wanted.

Mother did not buy another wedding ring; instead, she wore the one that had been her father's, my Canadian grandfather, wrapping thread around it to keep it securely on her finger. In time, the lost pounds came back, although I don't remember her ever dieting again. Then, as an old lady, she got quite thin once more and couldn't keep any rings on her fingers.

Several years after the loss of the ring, the August that I was getting ready to go away to college outside of Boston, I came home from working at the New Jersey seashore as a nanny for the summer, feeling nostalgic about leaving my orchard home. It was good to be back where the world was green with leaves and grass and even weeds, so I took a trowel and a basket and went out to work in the front garden. The soil there was light and dry from ashes that had been strewn along the gravel driveway in the years when the house was heated by a coal furnace. It wasn't hard to get my fingers around the roots of an errant grass tuft from the lawn, pull it out, and shake it free of dusty loam. Then, I noticed something small and round brought to the surface that wasn't a stone. It was a ring—my mother's wedding ring—clogged with dirt, but quite unharmed. I bore it in to her like a golden apple from the Hesperides.

In all my subsequent years of digging in gardens, I've never found another such buried treasure. But even if I found the gold of Troy, I know it would not have more meaning for me than that simple wedding band. It formed a link between me and my mother and gardens, enclosing me in the circle of a happy family.

Extending her influence and her love were the flowers transplanted from my mother's garden to mine—among them the early pink azalea. Mother also gave me two flowers that I had always thought were related: GARDEN or FALL PHLOX (*Phlox paniculata*) and DAME'S ROCKET (*Hesperis matronalis*), which isn't a phlox at all, but belongs to the mustard family. The phlox, as its names suggest, escaped from a cultivated garden and blooms in the fall. It has naturalized well in the wild garden, and although it is a tall and somewhat coarse plant, it is a pleasure to have there. It blooms in white or strong purple-pink, from July through October, when not much else is in blossom. Rocket comes earlier, often flowering in May. It has four petals, rather than the five of the phlox, white tinged with pale pink or lavender. The stems and leaves are smoother and weaker, and it has the long seedpods typical of the mustard.

Another flower from Mother is the WILD BLEEDING HEART (*Dicentra eximia*), a member of the fumitory family (the same family as Dutchman's-breeches). I used to call it squirrel corn, thinking that they were the same. But on closer examination, I see that the pink flowers of the bleeding heart are deeper in color, and they cluster at the end of the leafless stems rather than spread along the stem in the manner of squirrel corn blossoms. Also, wild bleeding heart will bloom all summer and into the fall, not just in the early spring. This graceful plant, with abundant, delicately cut silver-green leaves, makes a handsome show in a shady garden. It flourishes in my rock garden under the Atlas cedar and blooms happily in the wildflower garden, too.

Mother loved all flowers, and she almost always had some in the house from somewhere: her gardens, leftovers from arranging flowers for church or community affairs, wildflowers or grasses from the fields, or potted plants in the winter. However, out of necessity, I guess, she spent many more hours working in the big vegetable garden than she did among her flowers.

My dad would spread fertilizer and rototill the soil in the spring, but as the needs of the orchard increased with the season, most of the work of planting, tending, and harvesting fell to Mother. She was the one who gently put the special Martin's pole lima bean seeds into the pressed manure pots, watered them, and carried the trays of pots out into the warm spring sun and back in the house at night. She set out three green plants to each pole when danger of frost was past, and she carefully tied up the tendrils with strips of her old nylon stockings. It was this memory of the sprouting of bean plants that gave me the image for a little poem I wrote in a class I once taught on American poetry, a weak imitation of Emily Dickinson's style:

> You risen are from earth
> Bent back and heavy head
> To stand erect—at last—
> Unfolded Wings to spread.
>
> Other plans has the Gardener—
> He ties You to the Stake
> And watches You writhe upward—
> While leaning on His rake.

If there was a title, the *You* in the poem might be identified as a bean plant, or perhaps, ironically, a "human be'en," but Emily never gave her poems titles, and I haven't either.

When the time came for picking pole lima beans, I sometimes helped Mother on one side of a green wall of vines and me on the other. She wore a sort of homemade canvas sling bag for picking or, if she'd forgotten that, would knot up the corners of her apron to hold the bean pods and leave both her hands free. As we picked, we talked. I learned a lot from my mother in the bean rows, a lot about how to do a better picking job than I was doing, but much about other things too—a lot about life. Then, at the end of the row, she'd come round to check out my side for bean pods I'd missed, and to kill the woolly yellow grubs that I couldn't bear to squish.

If the beans we picked shelled out to more than enough for a meal, the smallest, most succulent limas were put aside for freezing. These were saved for Thanksgiving and Christmas. In later years, when I was married and had a family and my parents came to my home for holiday dinners, mother always brought her wonderful frozen lima beans as a contribution to the feast. Baby lima beans became my daughter Rachel's favorite vegetable. To this day it doesn't seem right to her to have turkey and mashed potatoes and gravy without lima beans. But the ones from the store aren't the same as the ones from her grandmother's garden.

In a way, the whole of the farm, orchard, meadow, and hedgerow was my mother's garden. In season, she would gather the fruits of the land: asparagus, escaped from the days when my grandfather had a truck garden; sweet wild strawberries, black raspberries, and blackberries along the fences; black walnuts from the tall trees along the bank of the stream; elderberries in the swamp; currants and rhubarb by the old woodshed, planted by someone who had farmed the place in a pre-Powell era. Nothing deterred her, not thorns or chiggers or poison ivy, which she took very badly. A hard worker, it pleased her to get something for no labor except the gathering. A saver, it tickled her to serve asparagus for which she hadn't spent a penny. Mother also garnered the fruits cultivated by my father, often picking them herself when he didn't have time. She liked the early transparent apples because they made the best applesauce, sour red cherries for pie, woolly quinces for jelly.

She did like a bargain. We sometimes teased her that she could talk people into giving her things that they wouldn't even sell to my father or me. But she was also very generous. Especially, she liked to give away things that she had made or grown herself. At Christmas, there were always decorated Mason jars of her home-canned fruit, golden peaches or ivory pears, waiting on the broad windowsill by the front door to be delivered to relatives and friends. Several everbearing red raspberry patches around Bryn Athyn started from her canes. She often gave lilac bushes to young couples landscaping their first home. In fact, the sweet-scented, old-fashioned lilacs in my own backyard are another heritage from my mother, who gave them to Bruce when he moved into this house in 1950. By the time I arrived in 1968, they had aged to old shrubs with thick, woody stems with a crowd of youngsters pushing up around them.

It was hard for me to watch my mother grow old and senile in her nineties; it was strange to see her just sitting in her rocking chair doing nothing and saying little. She had always been such an outgoing person. She loved a good cup of tea and a good visit with friends. And she had a lot of friends, many of them gardeners like herself. Even today, many years after her physical death, her love for growing things is still so strong in the house that her plants continue to flourish. Once in a while, my father remembers to dump a little water in the pots, but mostly they are neglected. Yet the African violets continue to bloom all year round. The Christmas cactus and poinsettia come to flower in their season. Dad was given a white geranium from the church at Eastertime, and it continues to flower many months later in the sunny kitchen window of the farmhouse.

Aunt Doris

The second woman whose sprightly presence I feel in my garden was one of my mother's good friends, and I sometimes went to visit her with mother. Doris was the youngest of seven sisters. The only brother, the eldest and doted on by all his sisters, was my husband's father. And so, when I married Bruce, Doris and her sisters became my aunts. What a windfall! They were wonderful ladies, those seven women, and I thought it a great privilege to be part of their family.

Once, Aunt Doris told me that the older girls in her family were never allowed to argue or express any disagreeable thought or feeling. At the dinner table, all had to be harmony and charity. But by the time Doris came along, a child born after her father's death, her mother had grown weary of suppressing her intelligent and talkative daughters, and the rules were relaxed. Doris and her youngest two sisters did have firm and independent opinions, which led sometimes to verbal disagreements, and that, Doris said with a twinkle, "Is why I'm so feisty." But these sisters remained the best of friends, even after they married and had children. They got together often, meeting for coffee in the morning to laugh and exchange news.

Aunt Doris had a gracious home, full of beautiful—if slightly uncomfortable—American colonial furniture, which I greatly admired in those days. On the lawn beyond the open porch at the back of the house was a sunken garden with every kind and color of stately iris. In bloom, they were magnificent. When she thinned them out, she was delighted to give extras away. For a while, I had several of her special varieties of iris planted around my house, but then they got borers. Even my high regard for my aunt didn't urge me to try to save them by digging up the rhizomes, poking out the beasts, and soaking the roots in a bore-killing solution before planting them out again. My love of gardening doesn't extend to doing much fussing, especially with poisons. If a plant grows, it grows; if not, I try something else. Maybe that's why I love wildflowers, because by their nature they are resistant to disease and pests. If they like the place you put them, they flourish; if not, they disappear without a trace. There's never such a messy death as borers.

Several of my wildflowers are transplants from Aunt Doris's woodland garden: foamflower, large white trillium, and two kinds of creeping phlox. Though long ago, now, I well remember her sprightly step, feet pointing out (the "Glenn walk," my husband called it) as she led Bruce and me to the edge of her woods, trowel in hand, talking, with her head a little to the side like a small, inquiring bird. "They say not to transplant a wildflower when it's blooming, but I say that's nonsense. How else do you know what you are getting? Just plant these today; don't let the roots dry out, and they'll be fine." She went on her knees and began to dig up some trillium. We'd brought a trowel too, but we were not to dig. She knew just what she was doing (implying that we would be in the way). Bruce and I stepped back. Under the tall trees, the green shadows were spread with white, triangular blossoms. The trillium seemed to glow with their own light, as if each flower were a three-pointed star. I've kept the enchantment of that sight down the years to inspire me in my own efforts at woodland gardening. The trillium she gave me have spread in my garden, but they don't look the same as my mind's-eye memory of those in her woods. They are lovely, but not bewitching.

LARGE-FLOWERING TRILLIUM, or *Trillium grandiflorum*, is a member of the lily family. This is a native perennial found in the woods from Canada to North Carolina along the East Coast. The three-inch bloom is bright white at first, turning pink as the days go by. Usually one flower, but sometimes two, appears above three large, dark-green leaves.

Samuel Gottscho says in *A Pocket Guide to Wildflowers:*

> Truly an artist's delight is the trillium's remarkable symmetry, determined by an unchanging "rule of three" three petals, three sepals, three leaves. It is common to all members of the genus, but none reveals it with greater beauty than the handsome *grandiflorum*. Whether in the woodland or in the garden, this regal trillium never fails to arouse the admiration even of those only mildly interested in flowers.
>
> **PAGES 123-124**

Visitors to my garden in May are happy to see the other blossoms, but when they come along the path to where these open white flowers are blooming, people always exclaim in delight, "Oh, look at the trillium!"

Of the two kinds of phlox that Aunt Doris gave us, one is WOODLAND PHLOX *(Polemoniaceae)*. The habit of this blue phlox is to creep along the ground in a humble fashion, then shoot up stalks with a few pointed leaves in pairs and burst into a small bouquet of sweet blossoms at the top. The pale violet-blue flowers, with wedge-shaped petals, radiate from the tip of the stem, which is somewhat hairy and sticky. It likes the open woods in the states that border the Great Lakes and from New York south to Georgia. This plant has been almost forced out of my wildflower garden by other stronger plants, but it has done well in the rock garden. Perhaps one spring I'll try to reestablish it in my woods by clearing a place in a spot that gets light and air and is relatively free of the persistent celandine and periwinkle.

The other plant, which I think Aunt Doris mistakenly called *Phlox divaricata* (perhaps because it has two kinds of leaves), I couldn't find stem nor stamen of in any of my usual books, under any name or picture. As well as the wildflower guides, I searched in my new, quite thorough book of over one thousand perennials to see if it had crept out of a tame garden by mistake. Then, in a series of booklets called *Wildflowers of Canada*, which I discovered at a used book sale recently, I found what I believe is the right flower. This series, printed in 1894–1895 by the newspaper *Montreal Star*, also includes wildflowers from the United States. These botanists (not named) identify the flower as CREEPING PHLOX (*Phlox reptans*). The illustration and written description certainly fit what I have growing in my garden. The plant has charming, rather wanton ways, growing close to the earth in a spreading patch of small oval leaves, reaching out for new ground with little curling tendrils, running off into the lawn or the path if I'm not paying attention. When the plant comes to flower, it throws up stems about six inches high with quite differently shaped leaves, pointed and narrow. Its blossoms have five petals, but they are broader than those of the woodland phlox and of a much richer hue, purple-blue with a golden dot in the center.

I like to think of this flower as the Glenn clan badge. Someone in the family, and it might have been Aunt Doris, planted this delightful flower years ago on the graves of her parents, Bruce's grandparents. Now it is moving sweetly up the slope to bind my husband's gravesite with family ties. I love having it in my garden along with the memory of a true lady.

Doris did have an aristocratic quality, interesting herself in public as well as private service. Although not a commanding figure in either stature or girth, she was not a woman whom one overlooked. She always spoke up for what she believed in. She was a committeewoman in Bryn Athyn for years, campaigning hard for candidates who would do a good, honest job at every level of government. Her interest in American history led her into endeavors to restore and salvage our architectural heritage. One fight she lost was to save a fine example of a Pennsylvania farmhouse that stood too close to where the Pennsylvania Department of Transportation was determined to widen Byberry Road at the crossing of Huntingdon Pike. How sad she was when the bulldozer crumbled the two-hundred-year-old fieldstone walls.

During World War II, she was an active member of the Church Military Service Committee, which sent out religious materials, letters, and packages to fighting men overseas. Perhaps her last act of devotion to her community and to our servicemen and servicewomen was to see that a fitting war memorial was made and erected in the Borough Park. She was particularly adamant that those who had fought and died in Vietnam should have a place as honored as the rest.

For almost as long as I knew her, Aunt Doris was the organist of the Bryn Athyn Cathedral. She retired only a few years before her death. It seemed a position determined for her by an act of God. As the story runs, the night that she got married, there was a tremendous thunderstorm. One bolt of lightning struck a pinnacle of the cathedral tower. The stone tip was knocked off, plummeted through the metal roof, and landed on the bench of the organ. Fortunately, the ceremony was over by an hour or so, and the wedding party, guests, and organist (who I think was one of her sisters) had all gone to Glenhurst for the reception.

When I picture Aunt Doris playing, I see her slim ankles and her trim feet in the worn slingback "organ shoes" moving deftly among the foot pedals. And yet, in the music that came forth, one was not aware of the organist. She had a way of subordinating technique to the spirit and purpose of the music that made one forget the player or even that the music was being played. The music just *was*. In her self-deprecating way, she always said that she was not a musician, but no musician who ever played or sang to her accompaniment agreed with her. My love of religious music came from her. Her pure rendition of the hymns and anthems in church allowed me to be fully absorbed in the affection of praising the Lord in song. There often does seem to be unheard music in my garden, but if I should be walking among the flowers one Sunday morning and clearly hear Handel's *Arioso* ("Thanks Be to Thee") soaring up and up as only Aunt Doris could play it, I will know that I have died and gone to heaven.

Phyllis

Phyllis was a kind and capable woman of the sort that once held society firmly together. She was able to do a lot of things well, and loved doing them all: wife, homemaker, mother, community volunteer, teacher, gardener. She was devoted to serving her church by bringing love to the neighbor into her practical life. She and her husband often entertained in their home, making newcomers to Bryn Athyn feel welcome. Phyllis headed up many a committee that made society suppers before the weekly doctrinal classes. Her suppers were very popular, as she was a good, old-fashioned cook who didn't spare the sugar or the butter.

Her creative energy was always evident in the classroom. She loved to put on plays with the children, emulating the way little children who have died and are growing up in heaven are taught lessons by means of plays or representations. These are carefully prepared, Swedenborg tells us, so as to be suitable to their tender minds and innocent affections. Although our earthly plays could not hope to incorporate such heavenly wisdom, Phyllis did select the plays carefully, so as to engage the children's better affections, giving them much innocent enjoyment and teaching them "knowledges" at the same time.

Phyllis's students also did a major project for every season. Diaramas with amazing detail were put together under her direction, one by each child: pipe-cleaner settlers and Native Americans eating the first Thanksgiving feast of modeling-clay food; Eskimos and igloos for a winter unit; biblical scenes, the Nativity for Christmas, and the triumphant entry into Jerusalem on Palm Sunday. The projects were far too wonderful and treasured to be thrown away, at least not until they were brown and derelict from ages of neglect in the attic. And if, over the years, one had several children go through her class, storage became a problem. One woman with a large family said—half laughing, half serious—that Phyllis should be made, every year, to take home one of each of her projects and find a place to keep it.

I believe that Phyllis had been a teacher in Ontario before she married and came to Bryn Athyn. She and my mother were both Canadian Kitchenerites of German extraction; in fact, I think they were distant cousins. They had similar characteristics, being hardworking, gregarious, generous women who loved flowers and people. As a young adult, I thought of Phyllis as one of my mother's generation more than mine, but through my daughter and the snowdrops, I began to consider Phyllis as my friend, and a gardening mentor. Her garden in the woods was a strong inspiration for my own wildflower garden, and she generously gave me a number of plants for it.

In those days, I was looking for ground cover and chose from her woods the WILD GINGER *(Asarum canadense)*. Peterson's guide informs me that it is from the birthwort family. Isn't that a curious name, *birthwort?* Interesting to think of plants having families and family names, heritages, and pedigrees, just like animals and humans. *Birthwort* seems rather lowbrow, but wild ginger is more properly identified as *Aristolochiaceae,* which sounds Latinate and most aristocratic. (Latin is always dressing up our down-to-earth

Anglo-Saxon words.) Both the plain and the fancy names seem to suit this plant. The large, rounded, leaves look like crushed and smoothed Chinese silk, but they hide a small, cup-shaped flower, reddish-brown, with three calyx lobes, low born in the crotch between two hairy leaf stalks that branch up from fleshy, underground stems. Gottscho's *A Pocket Guide to Wildflowers* informs me that "its dried roots were formerly used as tea to alleviate stomach-ache" (page 46).

The trouble with descriptions in flower books is that they never jibe exactly with the actual flower alive and well in my garden. Phyllis gave me several plants that she called WOOD HYACINTHS, or wild hyacinths. They bloom in three colors: blue, lavender-pink, and white, and they look similar to Dutch hyacinths (the kind that are forced for Easter), but are more delicate in color, leaf, and flower. The little bells are fewer; they don't gather into a tight cone but hang separately, as if they would ring if you shook them. Peterson is the only wildflower book I have that mentions hyacinths at all, and the picture opposite the text identification is not what I have, although there are some family characteristics. Peterson's wild hyacinths come only in blue, with six petals set in a more wide-open star shape; they grow in *southwestern* Pennsylvania and other states to the west of us.

Then, I looked up *hyacinth* in Johnson and Free's *The Concise Encyclopedia of Favorite Flowers* and found described, "a slenderer variety of the same species with fewer flowers" called the Roman hyacinth, which comes from the Mediterranean region. Perhaps this is my wild hyacinth—wild once in Italy. Whatever the variety, all hyacinths belong to the lily family and grow from a bulb, with several straplike green leaves and a sturdy stem on which the flowerets cling. All are fragrant.

Phyllis also gave me the WILD GERANIUM, which I found without difficulty in my guidebooks. This is a true cranesbill, so called because the seedpod looks like the long beak of that wading bird. It is native to the eastern United States and Canada, blooming from

May to June. The open-faced, five-petaled flowers are an inch or two across and soft magenta-pink. The leaves are light green, hairy, and deeply cleft. The plant grows about two feet tall with forked branches, and it seems fragile and sensitive. Although I read that, in the right location, this is profuse, I have never seen great quantities of this growing in the wild, and it does not easily spread in my garden.

Pulmonaria or LUNGWORT—the Latin name brings to mind my high-school study of anatomy: the pulmonary artery that feeds fresh blood to the lungs. This explains how the plant got the more common name of lungwort. It certainly must be in the same Boraginaceae family as Mertensia. In fact, many people coming into my garden in early to mid-March will exclaim, "Mertensia out already! But no, that plant's too short." The best I can tell from the picture and description in my garden handbook is that the plant I got from Phyllis is *Pulmonaria angustifolia*, which has a cultivated-garden origin. That means it is not a true wildflower, although it is excellent for the woodland garden. In habit, it is mat-forming. Its leaves are long, narrowly lance-shaped, finely hairy, and dark green without spots. The flowers are funnel-shaped and borne in terminal clusters, an intense clear blue at first, then tinted purple with age. I do love the bright blue of the flowers coming so early in the season before there is much color anywhere in the landscape. One can imagine Chicken Little seeing a patch of lungwort in March and crying out, "The sky is falling! The sky is falling!"

EPIMEDIUM is another plant from Phyllis that does not seem to be in the wildflower books. *Epimedium rubrum* grows to a height of a foot or so. It is self-contained, but an easy plant to divide; consequently, there are Epimedia in many places in the garden, like the silken tents of a fairy circus. The plant looks graceful because both leaves and flowers rise on very slender stems. The flowers are tiny, nodding in a breeze in loose, branched clusters, bright pink to crimson with yellow sepals in the middle. In my imagination, they look like small harlequins or tumbling acrobats in suits of motley. The leaves are almost as attractive as the flowers, heart-shaped with serrated edges, a variegated green in the summer, they turn bronze-red in autumn, and this color can last through the winter and into early spring if the weather isn't too severe.

More Gardeners

Several years ago, Beryl, a friend and down-the-road neighbor, gave me a few Epimedium plants that have an all-white bloom, and some with yellow outer petals and white trumpets, which remind me of miniature daffodils. These both may be varieties of *Epimedium pubigerum*, which I found described in *Perennials*. This plant flowers later in the spring, and the leaves are a uniform dark green until late autumn, when they also turn ruddy though not as red as Epimedium rubrum. The plants from Beryl have sparser growth and always look a bit delicate, as if they were in precarious health. Perhaps they need a change of scene.

Diane lives on a wooded lot that was once part of Aunt Doris's land, and she glories in the trillium that still flourish under the trees. Several years ago, she started an annual perennial plant exchange on her deck. Many of the gardeners in town, young and old, gather there each spring. We bring plants we've thinned out and carry home what we don't have in our own gardens. No buying and selling, just friendly sharing. Years ago, I got some WOODRUFF from Diane in a swap for forget-me-nots. The woodruff didn't do too well in the wildflower garden, but loves it among the herbs. A recent acquisition in my wild garden is a LENTEN ROSE, or helleborus, given to me by Diane. The Lenten rose was only planted out last summer. If it survives the winter and blooms, it should have a flat, pale green blossom tinging to pink or brownish-red.

Another newcomer in the garden that I'm waiting on is the TROUT LILY. My dear neighbor Mrs. G., who still gets down on the ground to weed at ninety-two, allowed me to dig some up from a patch on her lawn that came all of its own accord, as true native wildflowers should. I always get excited when the trout lilies bloom, and point out to her how delightful they are. My neighbor doesn't have too much patience with wildflowers. She prefers those plants that have a listing of *garden origin*. But there's no doubt that she's in the garland of good gardeners, with a green thumb for perennials, and a way with annuals that I don't have.

There used to be a wonderful garden club in Bryn Athyn. It had a lot of enthusiastic members: my mother, Aunt Doris, Phyllis, and Mrs. G. among them. They were all friends and neighbors who knew each other's gardens and were pleased to show off their own specimens and specialties with only a little benign rivalry.

Among the members of the garden club—and probably the most professional—were the Arringtons. Mrs. Arrington had been to a horticulture school and knew the Latin names for everything. Sometimes, when I'm looking up the botanical classification for my flowers, I think of her and wish she were here. She would have been happy to tell me, and far more interesting than a book. Mr. Arrington not only grew but propagated azaleas and rhododendrons. He had developed a beautiful white rhododendron, a new variety that he named after his wife. They had a greenhouse and little nursery as a sideline where they grew and sold shrubs.

One spring, on a trek round the Bowman's Hill Wildflower Preserve, Bruce and I were enchanted by the native azaleas blooming in the park. How delightful it would be, I thought, to have a golden-orange or soft yellow azalea in our garden. So we went to see the local expert on azaleas. That day, Mr. Arrington did not have any of the color that we had seen in the wildflower preserve, but he did have two deciduous azaleas of the same type with pinky-white blooms, which he called *appleblossom*. Being a child of the orchard, I couldn't resist the name, so we bought them and brought them home. We planted them with great care as befitted their origin and expense. For a season or two, they were lovely, but they did not long survive. The ghosts of those appleblossom azaleas haunt the garden still; I think that we planted them where the soil had too much potash from the burning of the trash. Anyway, they perished. Another azalea that we bought at the same time, a white one named *palestrina*, flourishes by the front door to this day.

The Arringtons had a beautiful wooded property; flowering shrubs grew all down one hillside below the house and into a green valley with a stream running through. Between the azaleas and rhododendrons were wildflowers: lady's slippers, trillium, and columbine. In the springtime, the garden seemed like poetry, and was the kind of garden that I liked to dream about having. But there were limitations on my dream I have no wooded hillside to work with, no green valley, no stream or water of any kind.

Late last summer, when I took my elderly father on an outing, we drove down the old Paper Mill Road. I wanted to see if I could find the country lane that led back into the woods to where the Arringtons once lived and had the nursery. I did find the lane, paved now but no less overgrown. From the turning-in of the driveway, I caught a glimpse of the garage and the greenhouses and went back in memory to when I used to visit there. But my dad and I didn't drive in. We don't know the people that live there now. I wonder if the garden is still as beautiful, but I fear that it is a thing of the past, a bygone dream.

Unfortunately, the garden club no longer exists, either. However, the gardening spirit in Bryn Athyn is still strong and growing, as seen in a wave of renewed interest in perennial gardening started by Danielle, a granddaughter of Aunt Doris's, who plants and maintains the cathedral gardens and helps people design gardens for their own property. And many of us continue on our own with our wildflower gardens.

This past November, I was sitting in a line of chairs in the Bryn Athyn Church School auditorium, waiting to donate my biannual pint of blood to the Red Cross, when another gardener, Eileen, came and sat beside me. I asked her how her woodland garden was doing. She laughed and answered, "Just what it should be doing this time of year—all died down." Then she asked me what I was doing. I told her I was trying to write a book about my wildflower garden. She exclaimed, "I didn't know you had a wildflower garden, too!" Till then, I hadn't realized that my garden was such a well-kept secret. However, like two people who find out through the secret handshake that they are members of the same club, we immediately had a lot to talk about while we waited.

As a young woman, Eileen was a wonderful dancer; at least I thought so when, as a third grader, I watched her perform for my ballet class. As a wife, mother, and grandmother, she has kept her talent alive by teaching ballet to children. When she was old enough, my daughter, Rachel (who'd always walked on her toes), joined Mrs. Roger's ballet class. Every week ordinary little girls would change from their jeans and sneakers into leotards and soft leather slippers for an hour or two and move their bodies to music, trying for rhythmic control in exercises and dance steps. In the spring, dressed in fluffy pastel tutus, they became in their imagination as beautiful as fairy princesses as they danced a story in recital for us: their parents, grandparents, and the older girls who had grown out of the ballet class, but came back to watch and to remember being ballerinas.

It was at the after-recital party held at Eileen's home for mothers and daughters that I discovered her wildflower garden. Wildflowers have the same qualities of fragility and reserve that we find in ballerinas; the same seemingly delicate restraint in both allows each the free spirit to blossom and to dance. On a windy day in the spring, I have often thought that the wildflowers looked as if they were dancing in my garden.

Eileen's garden had two features that I especially remember: the primroses and the pools. The pool near the house, fed by a little recycling waterfall, was big enough for waterlilies, surrounded by ferns and all shades of yellow primroses. It was like a color picture in a book of dream gardens. When Eileen saw how admiring a number of us were, she invited us to tour the rest of her garden on the hillside. As we climbed up the path behind the big pool and into the woods, we kept discovering other small pools catching the light and reflecting the greenery above. I was so enchanted that I asked if I could bring my husband and come back to see the garden again.

I was yearning for some reflecting water in my garden, so when Bruce and I visited, I asked Eileen specifically about the pools. She said that they were all man-made. All you needed, she said, smiling at Bruce, was a husband with a strong back and a spade to dig a basin. Then you lined it with black plastic; in the case of a small depression, a heavy-duty trash bag would do. Plastic in place, you filled the shallow hole with water, and lo and behold instant garden pool. The waterfall came about from a small electrically run recycling system. She encouraged us. We could do it.

Bruce and I went away feeling inspired and clever. But when we got home, practicality set in. Our woods shrank to a few trees; we realized that we had space for only one pool, and a small one at that. Our garden was far from the water spigot outside the back door. It was even farther from any electrical outlet that was needed for a pump to recycle water. I suppose we could have dug a trench and hired a plumber to lay a water pipe and an electrician to lay a line, but it did not seem worth the trouble and expense. After all, this was to be a little, natural, do-it-yourself garden, not Longwood. Bruce was happy to shovel out a shallow hole. We lined it with a trash bag, set stones around to hold the slippery plastic, and lugged buckets of water to fill it. We later laid some flat stones and planted primroses to make a primrose path. But try as I have with the pool and the planting through the years, it does not look like a picture in a garden book.

Eileen and I finished our supervised bloodletting for the Red Cross and had orange juice and a complimentary doughnut together. "Don't forget," she said as we got up from the table to leave the hall, "I want to see your garden. And you must come see mine again. Call me in the spring."

*Often, all the flowers seem to be in blossom at
once, and the garden is a millefleur tapestry of
shapes and colors.*

FULL-FLOWERING FAIR

AND THE SPRING AROSE ON THE GARDEN FAIR
LIKE THE SPIRIT OF LOVE FELT EVERYWHERE.

PERCY BYSSHE SHELLEY

We all acknowledge the universal sphere of love that pervades the world in springtime. Poets and songwriters prolifically celebrate the phenomenon of spring and love. Only the most winter-frozen heart would not respond to it. I attribute the rapturous simultaneous inflow into the realm of human thoughts and feelings and into nature's kingdom to a God of love and wisdom. When a person "makes an inward acknowledgement of God, which brings to life what he knows about God, his condition resembles that of a garden in springtime." So wrote Emanuel Swedenborg in *True Christian Religion* 457. Who could aspire to a more beautiful representation of his or her life than to be like a flowering garden in April and May?

In heaven, we are told, the spiritual sun shines always at the vernal height of warmth and light, and it is perpetual spring. On earth, we experience springtime conditions that are not so stable. Early April particularly can be most capricious.

Some people, and not only children, I suspect, think of the first of April as a day for fooling around and playing silly tricks on each other. Often the weather childishly plays along with the joke. Hal Borland, in his delightful book *An American Year*, calls April "a problem child month." There's such a fickleness of sun and shadow, you can't count on the weather for anything.

1994

APRIL 1

What a change from yesterday! This morning everything is dripping and sparkling in the sunshine after last night's heavy, cold rain. As I looked out my bedroom window early, early, I saw a pair of mallards walk pompously up the driveway, the male in the lead. They checked out the seed scattered under the bird feeder before moving on to look over the wetlands of our deluged backyard. I felt I ought to warn them that the water standing there was only a sometime thing. But by noon they were gone. I guess they had gotten the point on their own that this was not a place to nest. The nesting season will soon be here. The grass is on the green; tiny leaves are unfolding on the spirea bush almost before my eyes.

1997

APRIL FOOLS' DAY

This year, April came in like a bad joke. At least eight inches of wet snow draped itself over hill and dale like soggy cotton batting. Trees and bushes are bowed to the ground with the white weight. Under there somewhere are spring flowers. A breeze is stirring the trees; they move like vegetation under water, like ponderous elephants beneath burdens.

Stability doesn't seem to come after the month settles in, either. In my journals, I noted some of the ups and downs of mid-April weather:

1986

APRIL 13

Chill rain fell all this afternoon. Spring is on hold. We walked out around 6:00 P.M., when it was clearing to an April luminescence. Tonight, a thin moon hangs above the cold ground mist.

1990

APRIL 24

A day of temper tantrums—a humid morning brewed up thunderstorms that rolled around the sky all afternoon, but didn't clear the air.

> The uncertain glory of an April day,
> Which now shows all the beauty of the sun
> And by and by a cloud takes all away.
> **WILLIAM SHAKESPEARE, TWO GENTLEMEN OF VERONA**

It's true, just when it seems so glorious that I feel I have to be out in the garden and start for the door, the sun clouds over and another shower comes down. But that is part of the charm that makes April my favorite month in the wildflower garden. From late January on, with the coming of the snowdrops, the garden has been waking up, yawning and stretching. By the end of March, unless we have had exceptionally cold weather or too much snow, the eyes of the celandine are wide open, and daffodils are up and taking notice. But it is the warm days of April that bring the whole garden out of bed.

Several centuries ago, in the prologue to *The Canterbury Tales*, the English poet Geoffrey Chaucer sang:

> Whan that Aprill with his shoures sote
> The droghte of Marche hath perced to the rote,
> And bathed every veyne in swich licour
> Of which vertu engendred is the flour;
> Whan Zephirus eek with his swete breeth
> Inspired hath in every holt and heeth
> The tendre croppes, and the yonge sonne
> Hath in the Ram his halfe cours y-ronne,
> And smale fowles maken melodye
> That slepen al the night with open ye
> (So priketh hem Nature in hir corages):
> Than longen folk to goon on pilgrimages
> And palmers for to seken straunge strondes.

Chaucer's fresh and innocent April morning still stirs my deepest spring affections. However, unlike Chaucer's folk, I have no desire to seek strange lands, but only to make pilgrimages into my own garden.

First walk-through: *Morning, after breakfast or even before. There's a hint of cool mist in the air. The vegetation is wet with last night's shower, refreshed after unusual dryness for early April. The wild flower garden in its yellow period has been a joy this year—more daffodils than I ever remember. Now with celandine past its peak, and the yellow daffodils mostly gone, the creamy-white ones opening and the delicate, pale narcissus, the garden has moved into the white and blue period. Lungwort, grape hyacinths, blue violets, forget-me-nots, and mertensia bring down to earth the various shades of the spring sky. The sun, just breaking through the lingering clouds, sets every raindrop sparkling, lights up the white bloodroot blooms, and touches the Dutchman's-breeches hung out on their line to dry.*

Second stop: *Noon. I've been busy all the morning, but now I escape with my lunch into the sunny garden. The first wild yellow tulip has opened and is spotlighted by a sunbeam coming through a gap in branches, barely leafed. Catching sight of it from the bench brings me to my feet, applauding. While I'm up, I inspect the epimedium, which is adding a pink accent here and there. A bee is testing the rue anemone for honey value.*

Third visit: *Afternoon Tea. For a while, I sit at leisure on the garden bench sipping Earl Grey tea, pretending to be a lady of leisure. The early white butterflies dancing over the sweet blossoms entertain me, but before long, I'm up and walking round the paths, tea mug in hand, to see what else has opened or been brought up out of the soil by the warm sun. Ah, spring beauties. And phlox. But no sign of trillium yet.*

Fourth interlude: *Drinks before dinner. We bring chairs, so we can shift around if the strong light slanting in from the west is too dazzling when we sit on the bench. On his first garden tour of the day, my husband spots several trillium leaves curling up out of the ground with buds to follow. I'm sure they weren't there two hours ago, but I'm glad that he has the honor of being the first to see them. There's wonderful backlighting on the squirrel scuttling along the top of Homer's fence. Out on the lawn, the robins are singing for their supper, trying to entice the worms up out of the ground. The garden is lovely in the early evening and full of fragrance. We linger over our martinis, relaxing and exchanging the happenings of the day.*

Last walk-through: *Twilight. A little breeze has come up with the sunset. The pinks, greens, and blues have gone gray in the dusk, but the white blossoms are still soft statements against the darkening background. Like mysterious will-o-the-wisps, the tall narcissus nod and beckon. It is the end of an enchanted April day.*

Some of the flowers in the April garden you have already met. I've given their backgrounds, and told stories about where they were bought, or who gave them to me. Now, the time has come to learn about the others, which were gathered locally, from woods, orchard, meadow, and roadside. I must confess to violating Thoreau's good maxim: "I shall touch a hundred flowers/And not pick one." Not only have I picked flowers from the meadows and woods, but in stocking my wildflower garden, I have also dug them up root and all. There is a zookeeper mentality that wants to preserve endangered species; that says, this flower may perish in the wild. So, carry it home, plant and nurture it, and it will survive, multiply, and fill the earth.

Perhaps it was that noble thought, perhaps it was covetousness that caused me to take a trowel and small basket and capture a clump of BLOODROOTS I had seen on a bank along the road that runs past the cathedral. Bloodroots, like a lot of other wildflowers, seem to love banks. Unfortunately, I don't have any real slopes in my garden, but the bloodroots I dug up that day did take hold where I planted them in my garden. And I was justified in my thievery, for not long afterward a bulldozer tore away four feet of the bank where they had been growing to widen the road. If they'd still been in their natural place, the heavy blade would have annihilated them.

However, that wasn't the end of it, for this is a suspense story. After delighting the eye early each spring for years, the bloodroots were beginning to dwindle away, clogged by celandine and ivy and encroached upon by a spreading shrub. It seemed time to find them a new spot in the garden if I wanted them to survive, but it was a risky move. Many plants, like many people, don't bear too much re-locating. When next spring came, there were only two frail plants still alive, one in the old location, one in the new. Reinforcements were needed. Then one day, driving north toward Southampton along the Huntingdon Pike, I was just opposite the driveway into Glenhurst, the old Glenn homestead, when a flash of pure white on the other side of the road caught my eye. Bloodroots! Determined to have them, I returned later with my small, long-handled shovel and several pots, and abducted them, black gravel and all.

Did they survive? At first I feared not, for March came round and not a sign of them. But then, one warm April day, there were bloodroots in full bloom, as if they had sprung out of hiding when my back was turned to shout, "Surprise!"

I remember bloodroots from the open woodlands of my child-hood. Now there is such a tangle of vines in the woods that they are seeking a place on the roadsides instead, where tall trees come al-most to the verge and filter out the strong sunlight. The name of the plant, *Sanguinaria canadensis* (*sanguine* is Latin for *blood*) is a true description, as the sap in the stems and roots is as bright as arterial blood. The Native Americans, I am told, used the juice to paint their faces for war. The bloodroot, also a native American, blooms along the eastern seaboard from Canada to Florida and west as far as Nebraska. The lovely white flowers have from eight to ten petals with a cluster of golden stamens in the middle and roundish leaves with deep cutwork edges. Bloodroot is a member of the poppy fam-ily, which may explain why the flower shatters so easily, as poppies do. Once open, extreme heat, extreme cold, rough winds, or rough handling will drop the sensitive white petals to the ground.

There is one flower, pale pink, surviving still from Fromuth's, but the majority of the DUTCHMAN'S-BREECHES plants that are in the garden have spread from those that I gathered in the wild. Edgar Wherry includes under a description of their wild habitat in his

Wild Flower Guide: "rich woods along the eastern seaboard from Canada to Georgia," "wooded rocky slopes and stream banks" (Wherry 1937, 60). And that gives a clue to where the whitish-yellow ones in the garden were originally located.

Being romantically inclined, my husband and I loved to escape by ourselves once in a while for a weekend in Bucks County. We were lucky to have grown-up children still at home who were willing to look after the two younger ones for us. One of our favorite get-aways was the Inn at Philips Mill on Delaware River Road, above New Hope. It was while walking along the towpath of the canal one spring afternoon that we discovered the Dutchman's-breeches cascading down the canal bank and into the woods along the shore of the river. They were beautiful, and there were hundreds of them. A few would never be missed. Not expecting to garden that weekend, I hadn't brought anything to dig with. But that evening I lifted a soup spoon from the cutlery on our dinner table and dropped it into my purse. Next morning, very early, I stole out of the inn, across the wooden bridge, and down the towpath.

Bruce was just shaving when I returned with half a dozen plants wrapped in my scarf. He took only a weak stand for the environmental law against disturbing wildflowers; after all, I wasn't wantonly destroying them. I washed and returned the spoon to the dining room and didn't have a pang of guilt.

Wherry adds to his paragraph on Dutchman's-breeches that they "will grow in a wild garden, but bloom only sparsely." He's right on both counts. But I'm very happy to have them populating the garden, even if they don't have big families with lots of "breeches" on the wash line. They remind me of a beautiful, natural place along the Delaware River and a spring experience shared with my husband.

Recently, a woman who works with my daughter Rachel learned from her about my interest in writing about my garden, and loaned me an unpublished manuscript called *Flora's Clock* by Charles Louis Olds, a New Churchman and a homeopathic doctor, born in 1868. Dr. Olds writes about vegetables and flowers, trees and weeds with charm and a sense of humor. I was amused to read this rumination about his deceased wife's wildflower garden:

> At the foot of an embankment, and overshadowed by the branches of a noble maple, years ago my Beloved planted a little garden of the wildflowers of the forest and the uncultivated glades. It still exists, but barely. . . .
>
> I don't quite understand why we have such a passion for taming the wild things of the wild places and trying to domesticate them, but we do have that desire . . . we civilize them with our own brands of fertilizer and environment. And we expect them to like it, because we like it. And so they become anemic and spindling, and homesick for their own spot in the jungle.

There is truth to what the gardening gentleman (obviously of the old school), so wryly says. It is a bad human tendency to want to tame and possess things. I hope it is not my secret vice to desire to domesticate the wildflowers. "In wildness," as Thoreau wrote, "is the preservation of the world." I love to see the wild plants growing freely in "their own spot." But in these days of dwindling natural habitat and an increasingly polluted environment, we come to such sights less and less. The flowers may not grow as lushly in my small garden as they would where God, through nature, planted them, but they are alive and well, and that's something. And I never give them commercial fertilizer. Well—hardly ever. I do admit to trying to strengthen the heart of the wild yellow tulips once or twice with a bulb booster.

The YELLOW TULIP (*Tulipa sylvestris*) is in the lily family. It's another of those lovely flowers that came to us from across the sea. Being a bulb made it easy to transport in the dormant state. The leaves, few and narrow, come up first. Where there is only a single spear there won't be a flower, because that bulb is young and weak. Unassuming until it flowers, the tulip can then no longer hide its light under a bushel. It blooms like a burst of golden flame on a pale green taper about a foot long. Seeing a patch of these alight in the spring woods is enough to make you catch your breath. On our way to shop at a local department store one drizzly April day, Bruce and I spied just such a patch of wild tulips in the scrubby brush along Valley Road. We slowed down; we turned and went back to look more closely. Neither of us had ever seen such a sight before, although I suppose that they might have been there for years, and we'd never passed them at the blooming time. My heart yearned over those bright flowers.

Later, after supper, Bruce went out on his own and returned around dusk. "I have something for you," he said. "Call it a present for the anniversary of the April day I asked you to marry me." He handed me three wild tulips: bulb, leaves, stem, and flower in a clay pot. For his love of me, my husband had purloined those tulips at some risk of being caught at it along a busy road, although he did have some cover of coming darkness. I accepted the love, the remembrance, and the tulips.

The GRAPE HYACINTH is another member of the lily family that came to us originally from Europe. When I was young, we always called them bluebells, and sometimes I still do. The name *grape hyacinth* comes from their resemblance to a cluster of little grapes atop the stem, but the compact purple-blue flowers are open at the bottom and could just as well be little bells. When I was a child, the news would spread through the school, "The bluebells are blooming!" And in the afternoon, we would run to the field below the cathedral to gather handfuls to carry home. I have an impressionist painting—perhaps a Monet—hanging on the wall of my mind: a meadow full of gleeful children picking bluebells, and on a hill in the background, a tapering church tower.

1987

APRIL 8

It had been raining in the night, and was still cloudy and damp by mid-morning when Anne and I walked down Quarry Road toward Cairncrest. In the field below the church hill we looked for bluebells. We found some open, enough to stir up memories for me. On this chill day there were bird calls, but no shrill voices. I wonder if bluebell picking is still a rite of spring among Bryn Athyn schoolchildren.

Our family loved to take nature walks, especially on happy afternoons in the spring. One of our favorite walks was along the Pennypack Creek on an old track called Creek Road. Sometimes we got there by hiking up the abandoned railroad line from the Bryn Athyn post office, which had once also been a train station. Or we'd come past the cathedral, down the steep hill into Sleepy Hollow, and up again and along the road half a mile or more to the arched stone bridge.

When we came to the old stone bridge, however we got there, we always stopped to play several games of Pooh sticks. Bruce would count to three; we'd all drop our sticks on the upstream side and then rush to the other to see whose stick came out first. As the flow was sluggish, the outcome took a fair amount of waiting, but it was a pleasant way to while away a warm, lazy afternoon. Once, from the bridge, we saw a great blue heron flying away from us down the creek, and there were always mallards dabbling and ducking.

The bridge had been built to carry wagons back and forth from the busy paper and grist mills that used the Pennypack for water power. The mills fell to ruin years ago, but during the Revolutionary period, they were thriving. Historical hearsay has it that General Washington and his troops, retreating from the Battle of Germantown, marched through this area. Because of its historical and natural value, the Pennypack Creek watershed is now preserved as a natural wilderness by the Pennypack Ecological Restoration Trust.

It was across the bridge on the other side of the Pennypack, at the quiet corner of Creek and Paper Mill roads, that we discovered the wide swath of delicate blue flowers stretching from the muddy ruts at the edge of the road to the water. I forget the details of how we secured our specimens, but I think we came back later in the car with a shovel and containers. That was before all access into the park area by car was banned. The road was not being repaired anymore, and it was full of holes, but still passable, especially if one was eager to add a new flower to the garden.

And what was this pretty, mat-growing, shallow-rooted plant? Was it Jacob's ladder? While I was loosening up the soil and putting in the plants we'd carefully dug up by the creek, Bruce went to get the wildflower book. He brought it into the garden and made a careful comparison of book with plant. After a few moments he pronounced it: GREEK VALERIAN. We were grateful for Peterson's side-by-side pictures of Jacob's ladder and Greek valerian on the colored plate, and for his careful delineation of the minor differences in the descriptions. Both are in the phlox family, *Polemoniaceae*; both like wooded swamps and moist bottoms. Jacob's ladder blooms later (June to July), the stamens protruding beyond the blue-violet, bell-shaped flowers. The stems are taller and carry more paired leaflets, opening laterally off the stem like the rungs of a ladder. The leaves of the Greek valerian point slightly upward. The white stamens are tucked modestly away inside the paler blue blossoms until they are wide open.

What a delightful flower! Because it seems to be so at home wherever it touches down its roots, I have several patches spreading out in the wild garden and have transplanted some to other places.

A flower that grows freely everywhere is the VIOLET. When it comes to violets it's hard to tell "the garden proper" from "the garden improper," to quote from Charles Olds in his manuscript *Flora's Clock*. Violets of many kinds and colors appear out of nowhere in all the gardens and spill over the lawn. Sometimes I think we have more violets than grass. They are hard to get rid of—the knobby roots hang in there stubbornly, the leaves seem tough as shoe leather—but once, in zeal for a "decent lawn," we did try. In defeat, we surrendered ourselves to the delight of a lawn full of violets. For what is more delightful than the violet wherever it blooms? I still get a little thrill when I see the first shy violet of the spring season. For me, violets are synonymous with April and older than the naming of the month. They flourished long before anyone thought of mowing the meadows down to a greensward.

In his sixteenth-century herbal, Gerard talks at length about the wonderful properties of violets:

> The blacke or purple Violet doth forthwith bring from the root many leaves, broad, sleightly indented in the edges, rounder than the leaves of Ivy: among the midst whereof spring up fine slender stems, and upon everyone a beautiful flour, sweetly smelling, of a blew darkish purple, consisting of five little leaves, the lowest whereof is the greatest: after them do appear little hanging cups or knaps, which when they be ripe do open and divide themselves into three parts. The seed is smal, long, and somewhat round withall: the root consisteth of many threddy strings.

> ... many [people] by these violets receive ornament and comely grace; for there be made of them garlands for the head, nosegaies and poesies which are delightfull to looke on and pleasant to smel to, speaking nothing of their appropriat vertues; ... recreation for the minde ... for they admonish and stirre up a man to that which is comely and honest; for floures through their beauty, variety of colour, and exquisit forme, do bring to a liberall and gentle manly minde, the remembrance of honestie, comlinesse, and all kindes of vertues: for it would be an unseemly and filthy thing ... for him that doth looke upon and handle faire and beautiful things, to have his mind not faire, but filthy and deformed.

What a flower! The stuff of posies and "recreation for the minde," a plant for cleansing moral virtue, and also for healing the body:

> The floures are good for all inflammations, especially of the sides and lungs; they take away the hoarseness of the chest, and the ruggednesse of the winde-pipe and jawes, and take away thirst.

> There is likewise made of Violets and sugar certaine plates called Sugar violet, which is most pleasant and wholesome, especially it comforteth the heart and the other inward parts.

Small packages of these "plates" or tablets made of violets and sugar are still available from the Vermont Country Store catalog.

They are a favorite of my daughter, Rachel. I have sugared the flowers whole, myself; they are quite edible and look very pretty decorating a cake. The sugaring and eating of flowers for sweets was done in Medieval times, and into the time of Gerard and Shakespeare.

In England, the violet has been much prized through the centuries for all its "vertues," but most particularly for its sweet odor. Shakespeare sings it in many of his plays, as in these lines from *Twelfth Night*:

> O, it came o'er my ear like the sweet sound
> That breathes upon a bank of violets,
> Stealing and giving odour.

Fragrance does not seem to be one of the attributes of our native American violets; at least no more than a pleasant freshness is evident in the flowers that grow in my yard and garden. The lack of perfume and the fact that violets are so common may account for why the violet is not praised here in poetry and song as it is in England. Our COMMON BLUE VIOLET *(Viola papilionacea)*, called by Wherry "the dooryard violet,"—which he says "spreads by seed so rapidly as to become a weed" (page 69) is indeed a proficient sower. When ripe, the pod bursts open, scattering little seeds for several feet. Or so I am told. I never caught the plant doing it, though I've seen the open trisected pod and experienced the results of the casting of seed.

Besides there being a profusion of violets, there are also many kinds of violets. Wherry lists more than half a dozen varieties before he gives up. Peterson has brief descriptions of almost forty! In my garden, I have the common blue violet, of course, which comes in many shades of blue, from dark purple to pale azure. I have the SMOOTH YELLOW VIOLET and a branching white one that opens just a little later, called, I think, SWEET WHITE VIOLET. There is a pied blue and white, which I call Federal; it may be the same as someone else's Confederate. Then, I have a tiny lavender-pink violet with pointed elf-ears of leaves. This is the kind that grows in such profusion on the back lawn. The common blue prefers the front.

In the spring garden, one month merges into the other. Although some plants are supposed to come to bloom a little later than others, sometimes it is hard to tell early May from late April. Often, all the flowers seem to be in blossom at once, and the garden is a millefleur tapestry of shapes and colors.

Among the flowers that span the months of April and May are the SPRING BEAUTIES (*Claytonia virginica*) in the purslane family. A native perennial, the spring beauty grows from Canada to Georgia, and west even to Texas. But wherever they grow far and wide, I know just which remote green corner of my childhood orchard garden my spring beauties came from—a place where, in my mind, it is always spring. With the little brown stream meandering on one side and hoary old apple trees in bloom on the other, in a low place that is marshy after rain, the tiny pink and white flowers smile forever at the sun. I sometimes think of spring beauties as Garden of Eden flowers; they seem so blissfully innocent, never seeing anything dark or evil, for their eyes close when the daylight fades. Several candy-pink-striped flowers branch off the stem, but only one pair of linear leaves that look like grass blades. The plant is short, growing only about six inches high and often lying helplessly in a tangle because of its weak stems.

The one flower that rarely comes before its appointed month is the MAYAPPLE (*Podophyllum peltatum*) in the obscure barberry family. Although these plants wait until May to bloom, they push up out of the earth in April. I love the way the leaves are folded together like a furled umbrella, the flower bud making the round knob on the tip. As the stalk rises, the bud gets the full ripening power of the sun. Then the big cut-tooth leaves unfurl, two of them, and the bud, fastened into the fork, is tucked away out of sight in the shade. Part of my May Day morning ritual is searching under the twin umbrellas to see if any of the cuplike, waxy, white blossoms are open. If I find one or two, they add a special charm to the first day of the month.

The roots and leaves have poisonous properties, but the lemon-colored fruit or apple is edible. I've never eaten a mayapple apple myself; perhaps I shall try one this summer after it ripens.

The mayapple reminds me of maypoles, May baskets, and other ancient springtime customs. In the old days, people in England danced out at dawn to spend the first day of the month welcoming the advent of spring. Emulating the custom, if not the revelry, we made May baskets in second grade out of interwoven strips of green and yellow construction paper. The way the legend goes, you hang the posy secretly on the doorknob, where your true love will find it and be surprised and, oh, so delighted! I intended this posy for my mother, not having a true love in second grade. Early, early on the first of May, I remember getting up and creeping out of the house into the orchard to find flowers to fill my shallow basket. The morning sun shining through the mist turned it into a gossamer web between the trees. The grass was drenched with dew. I found some spring beauties and a few violets, but no mayapples. The paper handle was too short to fit over our kitchen doorknob, so I put the soggy paper basket on the porch in front of the door. Then, I was afraid that Mother would step on it when she came out for the milk, so I moved it to the side. Finally, I had to point it out to her, and when she did see the basket, I don't remember that my mother showed much delight. It was my wet shoes that she made a fuss about.

Funny how the little disappointments of childhood stay with us.

When I was in third grade, our class was to perform a maypole dance as part of the annual Spring Festival. Most of us girls loved it, but the boys, of course, thought it was awful, and the tomboys sided with them. Miss Erna, our gentle, elderly teacher, couldn't cope with the disparity of loudly voiced views. Consequently, the whole thing ended up in tears and a snarl of ribbons.

Only recently did I find out from Peterson's *Field Guide to Wildflowers* that the mayapple and the mandrake are the same thing. This may account for hearing faint echoes of the pipes of Pan when one is walking in places where mayapples grow, for the mandrake has all kinds of wanton associations. "Go and catch a falling star/Get with child a mandrake root," sang the poet Donne in his days of sowing wild oats. Gerard, in his herbal, makes a point out of discrediting the myths that the roots are forked in the shape of a man or a woman's body, that they flourish under a gallows, or that only a dog can pull them from the earth without harm. But Gerard does not discount their properties as a love or sleeping potion when boiled with wine, or as cause for "women to be fruitfull and beare children." Mayapples are prolific in more than myth. The many plants trying to take over in my garden came from a few long thick roots dug up in the woodland beyond the lower apple orchard.

The JACK-IN-THE-PULPIT is another plant brought from the woods of my childhood. But this preachy plant seems to stay where you put it, except for the ones that turn up in out-of-the-way places like wandering missionaries. These arise, however, not from any religious zeal, but from the seed carried in the bowels of birds and dropped under the white pines or other roosting trees.

In the arum family—the same family as the skunk cabbage— there are three kinds of jacks, all native to our area. I think that the one I have is the woodland jack-in-the-pulpit. My two guides, Wherry and Peterson, do not agree on its Latin name, whether it is *Arisaema atrorubens* or *Arisaema triphyllum*. Sorting it out might make for an interesting botanical dispute among experts; as a lay-woman, I don't care much about the outcome because I prefer the common name anyway. And it is an interesting name. *Jack* was a generic term for one of the masculine gender, a peasant or man of the people, not of the upper classes or the learned, like a priest. One would not expect to find jack in the pulpit unless there was a social upheaval or an ecclesiastical revolt. So is there a history here? The name reminds me of the nursery rhymes that have political references in their verses.

The hooded pulpit rises a foot or more on a central stalk flanked by two three-part leaves in the same sheath, but each having its own stem, flecked with dark purple. The white-robed preacher stands tall and substantial under the canopy, which is green on the out-side, lined with deep purple and a pattern of light tracery inside. The actual flowers of the plant are like a cushion for his feet. In the autumn, when the spathe and the leaves die away, the fruit of the plant, a bunch of bright red berries, stands revealed. I suppose the red color is to catch the eye of birds and beasts that might miss it otherwise in the dim woods.

Another plant with a cluster of red berries in the fall is the SOLOMON PLUME or FALSE SOLOMAN'S SEAL (*Smilacina racemosa*). The oval, pointed, and heavily veined leaves climb alternately up the limber stalk, which terminates in a tight spray or plume of foamy-white flowers. This is a showy bloom as much as two feet from the ground. True SOLOMAN'S SEAL (*Polygonatum commutatum*) is similar in leaf form and arching stem, but the flowers of this plant don't bunch up at the top; but they grow along the stem from the leaf axils in slightly yellowish, double bell-like blossoms. Later in the season, its dangling berries are blue. Both of these flowers bloom in my garden, but I never knew why one of these plants was labeled false and one true until I got to the root of the matter. The reason is that the impostor does not have the seal-like scars on its underground stem that identify the true heir. Both are on the same family tree—the lily family. They are close relatives of the LILY OF THE VALLEY, of which I have a few in the wild garden and many more in the rock garden under the Atlas cedar.

There is another flower that I have transplanted into my garden from the wild—the STAR-OF-BETHLEHEM. It sends up its bright green grass tuft of leaves every year, but won't bloom. Perhaps this steril-ity is symbolic, but I don't like thinking so. I'd rather think that it doesn't like its location, and not that it shows any lack of faith on my part in following Christ's star. Where it does bloom, the low plant has a lovely six-petaled, star-shaped blossom that is bright white. It seems to prefer roadsides and gravelly places to wood-lands, yet the most beautiful one I ever saw was in our shaded church cemetery.

1994

MAY 29

In the late afternoon I walked to the wooded cemetery and planted a few of the pansies that Bruce loved on his grave. In another month there will be too much shade for pansies, but if the deer don't eat them they may bloom for a while. The mowers had been there and cut down the forget-me-nots; only the creeping phlox escaped the blade. As I was walking away up the path, I was startled to see a star-of-Bethlehem in full bloom. It was shining white. I didn't know how I had missed it on my way in, for it was at the edge of the parking area where a tire had pushed it up on a hump of earth and gravel. In such a precarious place it wouldn't survive crushing long; it was too beautiful to let perish. I took my trowel and dug it up into two clumps. Rather than take them away and plant them in my garden where they might never bloom again, I decided to plant one for Bruce and one for Lyris Hyatt, Bruce's first cousin, in remembrance of her poem "Synonymies of Spring."

When I got home I looked up the poem, and in so doing, I reflected a moment on the woman who had been my teacher, friend, and colleague. In these lines from "Synonymies of Spring", Lyris caught part of her earth life and a glimpse of heaven:

> Not your robin in February,
> huddled glum on the apple branch,
> nor blood-red buds of the silver maple
> swelling gallant in a blue March sky;
>
> but in the gutter, dry or sodden,
> almost hidden in the gravel,
> here, these pearl-size ivory bulbs,
> through all the rains or drought of April,
> put up with it. They wait it out.
>
> > To startle a morning,
> > from them will stem
> > six petals, white
> > and subtle, bright:
> > the mid-May Star-of-Bethlehem.

All the months of April and May I have been in a kind of "gutter" and now, having waited it out, up springs life from the gravel—a resurrection. Two days ago, on the anniversary of my husband's physical death, I woke up with such a sense of joy that it startled my morning like a bright flower. Finding the star-of-Bethlehem today and planting it by the headstone of the poet was a tribute to the power of art to make meaning of my experience.

I love my fragrant May garden, sweet with lilac breath. To wander through it on the quiet paths is to feel the tranquility of heaven. The garden is full of light, caught and held by the floating white dogwoods overhead, the glowing and grounded trillium, the sprays of white wood hyacinths rising like fountainheads from their pools of green leaves. The azaleas, too, are luminous, like lavender-pink clouds at sunrise. When I am in the garden on a sunny day, I think of the impressionist painters and what they were trying to do with blobs of color and with light.

The colors of the May garden are white; the true blue of forget-me-nots; the various tones of lavender-blue in Greek valerian, phlox, and wood hyacinths; lavender-pink of wild geranium, pale pink spring beauties, deeper pink of wild bleeding-heart. Deep pink outlines the leaves of the epimedium. Here and there are touches of yellow: violets and the last of the primroses by the shadowed pool, a buttercup where the sun is strongest. And all are buoyed by the green of leaves and softened by the fronds of ferns.

Birds are so much a part of the spring that it is incomprehensible to think of having a garden without them. What a thrill to hear the first high, thin whistle of the white-throated sparrow. My son Thane once told me that song meant spring to him, and it's what I think of when I read e. e. cummings's lines about a goat-footed balloonman whistling.

Of course, there are some birds that stay with us all year round. The cardinals and chickadees are our familiar friends. Others, like robins, we've come to expect back early every spring. We love robins, but it is the unusual visitor that really tickles our fancy. And there is nothing like a chatty little wren to brighten up one's life. Some years after Homer put up the fence between our properties, Bruce used it to nail up an old birdhouse that had once been mounted by the front door. He'd taken some care to clean out the spiders and refurbish the place. I don't think anything happened that season, because the next spring he posted a "For Wrent" sign, in case wrens just passing through thought the house was already occupied. We may have had some nibbles after the sign went up, but no takers, for in my journal I find this entry:

1988

MAY 11

On Saturday Bruce took out his paintbrush and added "Cheep" to the "For Wrent" sign by the wren house on the fence. Today we noticed that a pair of wrens seemed to have closed the deal and were moving in. We read in a bird book that the jenny wren is hard to please. Sometimes johnny will arrive in town, choose a location, and begin to build a nest, but when his wife comes, she may veto the whole enterprise. We are hopeful, because there were two of them carrying in the furniture.

I can't find the entry in the journal that verifies it, but I think the wrens did make a home in the birdhouse and raise a family that year. Then in a later year I wrote:

1990

MAY 25

While sitting with drinks on the patio, we watched a little wren hopping along the top of the fence and checking out the birdhouse. What a racket that small bird can make! At that moment, whether jenny took our wren box seemed like the most important thing in the world, Bruce said.

JUNE 1

Wrens have moved into the little old birdhouse on the fence. As Bruce went by with the noisy lawnmower today, he was fixed by a bright, accusing eye from the hole. There is so much chatter everywhere, all day, that we feel as if wrens have taken possession of our whole yard.

By the middle of June there were fledglings, for the parents began winging back and forth across the yard, popping in the hole and out again. As landlords, we watched with proprietary interest from the patio the unceasing food flights: to and fro, hunting down an insect, carrying it back, and stuffing it into a hungry mouth. It was a tremendous effort, but the airlift was successful. In a week or two, three small wrens, tails up, emerged and perched on top of the fence, ready for flying lessons. By this time, spring was over, and we were well into summer.

Ferns are an intriguing, ancient kind of plant life,
leading us back through eons to the primeval ooze;
they flourished long before plants had flowers,
fruits, or seeds.

RABBIT, RABBIT

HE WHO PLANTS A GARDEN, PLANTS HAPPINESS.
CHINESE PROVERB

If, on the first day of the month, you say, "Rabbit, rabbit," when you wake up, it is supposed to bring you good luck. It's like wearing a rabbit's foot, I suppose. How rabbits got to be associated with good fortune I don't know. Perhaps it came into the West from China where they celebrate a year of the rabbit and set a lot of store by fortunes, even tucking them into their cookies. Anyway, wherever it came from, my children and grandchildren liked reciting the incantation and inviting a month's worth of happiness.

1989

MAY 1

Rabbit, rabbit! No need to conjure them up, they're all over the garden, fat and sassy.

1992

JUNE 1

Rabbit, rabbit, or "Bun-nee, bun-nee," as my little grandson Laird says. This spring, the yard is full of bunnies, much to his delight. When we spotted one from the window at breakfast time, he was gleeful and wanted to get down from his high chair immediately and "get it." It's amusing to watch them running around the lawn: Laird on his fat little legs, the rabbit hopping a few paces to see if the boy is serious about the chase, then scooting and zagging and waiting for him to catch up, then off again, as if the rabbit enjoyed the game as much as the child. Laird and his mother, Cara, are visiting from South Africa, where there are no bunnies like ours. My home in Pennsylvania is tame in comparison to a land of exotic beasts like giraffes and elephants; I feel fortunate to have the means of so delighting the little world traveler with the rabbits in my garden.

Rabbits and children seem to belong together. Writing about Laird and the rabbits made me think of *When We Were Very Young*, A. A. Milne's poem about a little boy looking for a rabbit here, there, and everywhere.

Children's literature has done a lot to make rabbits appealing through poems and stories that touch every season. Alison Uttley wrote many stories about Little Grey Rabbit, a delightfully practical, charitable, and self-effacing English lady rabbit. My favorite is *Little Grey Rabbit's Christmas*. Every year on Christmas Eve, part of our family's ritual was to listen to my husband read this story aloud. I still miss him singing the carol at the end, "Holly red and mistletoe white," in his pleasant bass voice. He also would often read the chapter from *The Wind in the Willows* that describes carolers coming to Mole's house in the snowy forest at yule tide.

There is great charm in stories about animals. They speak directly to our affections, particularly those about cute animals like rabbits. Off the top of my head, I can't think of any story where the rabbit is the villain, from *The Velveteen Rabbit* to the stories of Brer Rabbit; soft and cuddly, wily and wiry, naive or sage, in fiction, the rabbit always has us on its side. Even A. A. Milne's rather bigoted and self-important Rabbit in the Winnie the Pooh stories earns our sympathy when he gets lost in the fog at the top of the forest and becomes "a sad and sorry Rabbit."

Unlike my small grandson Laird, who is single-minded in his adoration, I'm of two minds about rabbits. They are cute. They can also be destructive. I guess that's the gardener in me speaking, for sometimes I fire up just like Mr. McGregor with an urge to run after them brandishing a hoe.

1987

FEBRUARY 28

The last day of the month—our first little yellow crocus opened to the sun this morning! But our joy was short-lived; a rabbit nipped off the flower.

1989

APRIL 9

*From the bathroom window this morning, I watched a fat rabbit hop out
of the herb garden after finishing off the second row of blue violas. It is
maddening to watch her gobbling up the flowers, but it's too early in the
morning to go chasing out into the yard. This rabbit is both voracious
and tame, not at all afraid of the hand that feeds her. I'm sure she thinks
we're providing all these specialties just to satisfy her appetite.*

APRIL 12

*Our fat brown rabbit has been joined by another fat brown rabbit. They
were romping on the back lawn early this morning while I was down getting the morning tea. Fun to watch, and I suppose if one can't lick 'em,
one might as well enjoy 'em. I fear the tulips don't stand a chance, not
with two to decree, "Off with their heads." I put a piece of rusty chicken
wire I found in the garden shed around the wild tulips to see if I could
save them this year.*

APRIL 22

*Took my lunch into the sunny wildflower garden to enjoy the one wild
tulip the rabbits have allowed to stand and unfold itself. The really infu-
riating thing is that the rabbits don't even eat tulips; they behead the
flower and leave it. When the tulips are demolished, that's it for another
year; they don't retrench and bloom again. Because of the rabbits, I've
about given up tulips, except for these wild ones.*

The two rabbits I saw together on the twelfth of April may be
what led to the rabbit nest that I found later in the summer in the
middle of a thick patch of oregano in the herb garden. The hollow
in the earth was lined with dried grass and soft fur to cuddle the
young. But the baby rabbits had gone. In spite of my feelings about
rabbits who make a breakfast of my flowers, I was sorry to have
missed them. I hope they weren't prey for one of the many cats or
dogs that meander uninvited through our property.

My animosity toward rabbits never extended to using dogs, BB-
guns, traps, or poison, and never lasted long. Rabbits are, after all,

God's creatures, living in the order of their lives. They can't really be blamed for eating. Once one gets over the notion that one is growing pansies or crocuses for one's own benefit instead of for the sheer love of growing them, harmony can be restored between gardener and rabbit.

One can't talk about rabbits and children and gardens without thinking of Beatrix Potter, an English author and a naturalist of sorts. Drawing on her experience and her imagination, she wrote three classic rabbit stories: *The Tale of Peter Rabbit*, *The Tale of Benjamin Bunny*, and *The Tale of the Flopsy Bunnies*.

Every spring, *The Tale of Peter Rabbit* was acted out in Phyllis's garden by her first graders. With a lot of help from her husband, the garden scene was set with all the accurate props. A little vegetable patch, a glassless window frame with geraniums for Peter to knock over, a gooseberry net where he wrestled out of his jacket, a low birdbath for a pool with a goldfish swimming in it for the occasion. The children took the parts of the animals, dressed up in charming costumes made by their clever teacher and mended, cleaned, and pressed each year by fond mothers. All the characters from the book were there: Mrs. Rabbit and her family, the white cat, the mouse with the pea, the birds. One child—usually the best reader—narrated the story, reading right from the book with all the hard words while the rest supplied the action. The tallest boy in the class played a crotchety Mr. McGregor. The role of Peter was given to the class ham, who gleefully made the most of his chance to show off legitimately.

It was great fun. As Mr. McGregor chased Peter round the house shouting, "Stop, thief! Stop, thief!" all the little brothers and sisters sitting on blankets on the grass giggled. Everyone cheered when Peter squeezed under the gate unharmed, especially his mother, who had been a little nervous about Mr. McGregor's flailing hoe.

Although I haven't had a first grader for a long time, I remember clearly perching on a folding chair in the May sunshine with the other parents and grandparents enjoying the children, who were having such a good time. At the end of the play, there were refreshments: rabbit-shaped cookies and punch for everyone. Then Phyllis made a special presentation to each child in the class: a *Peter Rabbit* coloring book with the original Beatrix Potter illustrations. The boys and girls often gave her commemorative gifts, too. She collected so many Peter Rabbit things over the years that she set up a special room in her house to hold them.

I think that many people with fond memories of those plays thought the saddest thing about Phyllis's retirement from teaching was the end of Peter Rabbit in the garden.

1994

JULY 30

Phyllis died Friday, and her resurrection service is on Sunday. In thinking and talking about her today, Rachel and I remembered all the wonderful projects and plays she did with the class. I remember, too, how she gave me plants and encouraged me to start my own wildflower garden. Thinking about Phyllis and her garden renewed my intention to write a book about gardening and what it has meant in my life.

I noted, when next I visited the cemetery, that a small garden statue of a rabbit had been set up on Phyllis's grave beside her headstone. It seems exactly right.

Every garden, to be a real garden, needs to have children to play in and enjoy it. Their delight brings a special sphere and seems to radiate from the trees and flowers. In *Heaven and Hell*, paragraph 337, Swedenborg describes a living picture, in which young children in a garden in heaven have a happy time while receiving instruction:

> I have been permitted to see children most charmingly attired,
> having garlands of flowers resplendent with most beautiful
> and heavenly colors twined about their breasts and around
> their tender arms; and once to see them accompanied by their
> teachers, in a park most beautifully adorned, not so much
> with trees, as with arbors and covered walks of laurel, with
> paths leading in; and when the children entered, the flowers
> over the entrance shone forth most joyously. This indicates
> the nature of their delights and how, by means of pleasant and

delightful things, they are taught the nature of innocence and charity, which the Lord continually instills into these delights and pleasures.

Perhaps it was this spiritual concept unconsciously flowing into the memory of the ways Phyllis had shared her garden with happy children that inspired me to invite my granddaughter Jenna Lynn to bring her fourth-grade class to my wildflower garden. Jenna's teacher, Miss Rosemary, who has all the English love of flowers and gardens, was most enthusiastic. She was teaching a unit on wild-flowers that spring, and we timed the children's visit to the garden to complement what they were learning in the classroom. The date was set for a day in late April, when, ideally, the weather would be warm and all the flowers blooming.

I worked like a Trojan (an expression borrowed from my mother) in the garden early that month to make it as beautiful as possible. My family teased me that I acted as though I was trying to win the grand prize for a wildflower exhibit at the Philadelphia Flower Show instead of entertaining a group of nine- and ten-year-olds.

My garden isn't very big, and even with some widening, the paths didn't allow much more than one or, at best, two small people to see the same flower at the same time. How could I make a tour interesting for fifteen kids? Lecture seemed to be a dull approach to the flowers. Instead, Bruce helped me to prepare a flower identification game for the class that we hoped would encourage the children to spread out and discover the flowers on their own. I selected the descriptions and pictures—from my Peterson and Wherry wild-flower guides—of eight different and fairly common flowers the children might have seen before, which were currently in bloom (cross my fingers) in my garden. Bruce photocopied the illustrations and descriptions (probably violating copyright law) onto a sheet of paper, front and back: rue anemone, trillium, wild yellow tulip, Dutchman's-breeches, mayapple, mertensia, Greek valerian, and spring beauty.

Late in the afternoon of the day before the fourth grade came, I dug up enough small plants (those I had many of) and potted them so that each child could choose what he or she liked best and take one home.

How disappointing it was to wake up on the appointed day to the uncertainty of a dark, cloudy morning. It had been raining during the night. Would it rain again? The teacher called, we conferred, and we decided to chance it. I donned my green slicker and went out into the wet garden. Miss Rosemary, carrying her British umbrella, arrived with the class. The children were enthusiastic to have an outing, even if the day was damp and chilly. We did a quick walk-through of the garden first, before I explained the game plan. Each child got a separate sheet, but we encouraged working in pairs or threes, helping each other, because it would be less competitive, more fun, less of a task. There were two rules: stay on the paths and don't pick the flowers. The children began scampering through the garden, noses twitching like rabbits.

Watching them, I was reminded of something Aunt Doris, a wise woman, once said about the importance of letting children discover nature on their own. Adults, even teachers, have to guard against taking away the joy of interaction between a child and the created world by always being the one to tell, to point out, to itemize and order. There is something wonder-full about innocent ignorance and the freedom to explore. One of the treasures of my young days was the freedom of seemingly endless afternoons of discovery out-of-doors. I thought how lucky these children were to be out this morning in the fresh garden, even though it was a school excursion in a contained area. How lucky they were, and I had been, to grow up in this community with access to so much open space and natural beauty.

When the children found a flower in the garden that matched one on their sheet, they put a check by it, and when they had checked all eight, they could bring their sheet to Miss Rosemary or me and then choose a plant as a prize. One pretty little girl who had moved slowly along the paths and taken her time to find all the flowers came up last to claim her plant and was disappointed not to see the kind of flower she liked best left on the bench. It was my pleasure to take the trowel and dig her a bright yellow violet and send her home happy.

That night I wrote in my journal:

1986

APRIL 22

Jenna invited her fourth-grade class to come and enjoy the wildflower garden today. We got dismal weather, not the warm sun that would have made it perfect, but I'm glad we went ahead anyway, in spite of the threat of rain. And fortunately, the shower held off until they started back to the classroom.

I was proud of my garden; everything looked fresh and pretty. It was a happy morning for me and, I think, for the children. Even those that weren't too enthusiastic about the flowers politely said thank you, and everyone liked the cookies.

The story is that those cookies were invented by an old man, Uncle Joe, who lived in Marblehead. The big, flat cookies were supposed to resemble the frogs in Uncle Joe's pond, hence the name *Froggers*. Actually, they look more like lily pads to me. Whatever. They have become a traditional favorite in our house, and all children seem to like them. The big size is part of the appeal, as is the sweetness. This recipe comes from the Publick House, Sturbridge, Massachusetts.

JOE FROGGERS

2 cups sugar	1-1/2 teaspoons cloves
1 cup vegetable shortening	2 teaspoons baking soda
7 cups all purpose flour	1-1/2 teaspoons salt
1 tablespoon ginger	1 cup water
1 cup dark molasses	

Cream the sugar and shortening. Put the soda into the molasses. Sift together the dry ingredients. Add alternately to the creamed mixture the dry ingredients, water, soda, and molasses.

Roll out the dough on a floured board to 1/4-inch thickness. Cut out cookies with a large, round cookie cutter (I use the top of a small funnel). Makes about twenty five-inch cookies. Wash the tops of the cookies with milk. Bake 10 or 12 minutes at 375° degrees.

How often the taste of good food is associated with a pleasant experience, and feasting with a holy day, like Christmas. This comes from the spiritual representation of food, of course, and that is why there is so much reference to eating and drinking in the Bible. When Jesus fed the five thousand in the wilderness, it wasn't just natural loaves and fishes that he gave them, but spiritual food to satisfy a deeper hunger.

Of course, the fourth graders who enjoyed the flowers and the cookies that April day weren't the first children to grace the garden; my own two had been in and out since they were little, playing imaginary games with friends or musing alone, often joining their elders there for lunch, or tea, or "special" drinks. The Easter Bunny hid colored eggs among the flowers there, as well as all over the yard, for our annual family egg hunt. The wildflower garden was part of our lives. It was something I knew was vital for me, but thought everyone else took for granted. Therefore, I was surprised and pleased when my son, Thane, announced one day that he was going to do his sophomore science project on the wildflower garden. Did I think that was a good idea?

1988

JUNE 1

Thane had to know if there were fifty species of plants in the wildflower garden—flowers, trees, weeds, et al.—so I went out to take a survey and wrote down most of the plants I could still see above ground or remember. (By June, some of the flowers, like mertensia, are only a memory, just melted away. Unless you know the garden well, you'd never know they had ever been there.) Without straining or counting different varieties of things like violets, I found sixty. Amazing what one small area can produce.

I still have the three-by-five-inch scraps of blue-faded-to-gray scratch-pad paper folded into the leaves of the 1988 journal on which I made my survey list.

JUNE 7

After great labor—way into the night—Thane finished the project with reference help from his parents. Bruce brought some fern books from the library, and we spent one lunch hour this week researching ferns at the table. Rachel got to laughing. She said, "You might think my parents spent their life identifying ferns. You and Dad are really versatile." It's true we are interested in lots of things, partly spurred on by our children's educational needs. The next lunchtime we devoted to a discussion of the Reformation and Renaissance in preparation for Rachel's history test.

I wish that I had Thane's finished botany project. He had even drawn and colored a general plan of the garden, which I would love to have and cherish. But he handed it in, got his grade, and never retrieved the project. When I inquired after it, he said, with the unconcern of a teenager, that if I wanted it I could ask the teacher for it. So I did. The teacher seemed almost as unconcerned as Thane. Although he didn't say so, I think that he might have thrown it out; anyway, he didn't have it at hand and was disinclined to look for it. It's one of those lost, irreplaceable material things that I feel frustrated and sad about at the same time. This is the feeling that drives me into the attic or the back of closets to rifle through piles of things on shelves or shuffle through the contents of boxes and trunks. What I'm missing just must be there somewhere. Often, what I wanted so desperately and didn't find turns up later, after I have stopped looking for it. But I know that this record of my wildflower garden never will.

The research we did on ferns went by the board also, as I never wrote it down. Now, ten years later, when I need information on my garden ferns, I have had to go to the library again. Between Edgar T. Wherry's *Guide to Eastern Ferns*—which I studied before lunch in the library—and a charming book published in 1899 by Frances Theodora Parsons, titled *How to Know the Ferns: A Guide to the Names, Haunts, and Habits of Our Common Ferns*—which I brought home to digest with my roast beef sandwich—I think I have identified the varieties in my garden. There aren't very many. Now that I've dipped into the study, I find my interest awakened, as Frances Parsons assured me it would be. Ferns are an intriguing, ancient kind of plant life, leading us back through eons to the primeval ooze; they flourished long before plants had flowers, fruits, or seeds. Ferns multiply along the root stalk or by spores borne on their fertile fronds. I am eager now to try to collect some other kinds and add them to the garden. One of my next-door neighbors has the handsome ostrich fern in her woodsy backyard; perhaps she'll give me some root stock if I ask nicely.

When Thane did his science report, there was a fern in the garden that seems to have recently disappeared. At the time, we typed it as a brittle fern, I think, perhaps Wherry's LOWLAND BRITTLE. It was a low-growing fern, less than a foot high, and, as I recall it was a silvery-gray color when it first came up in the spring and then developed rusty-brown edges. This fits the description of the RUSTY WOODSIA in Frances Parson's guide. The drawing in her book also looks familiar. The fronds are oblong, lance-shaped; the pinnae are cut into oblong segments with an almost lacy appearance. But without the fern to work from, I feel tentative about making any identification. I remember it was purchased from a nursery and did not come naturally into the garden as the other ferns did, so it may not have been suitable for my garden, and so it died out.

In his *Guide to Eastern Ferns*, Wherry tells me that the HAY-SCENTED FERN was first discovered in Canada and mistakenly classified as *Dickinsonia pilosiuscula*, which is, in fact, how Parsons listed it in her earlier book. The later botanists, Wherry among them, identify it as *Dennstaedtia*. Who knows? Perhaps by now it has been reclassified again.

The hay-scented fern, which looks just the way a fern should look, comes up in the late spring in fiddlehead curls covered by the palest green fuzz. In fancy restaurants, these are sometimes on the menu as a delicacy. When mature, the fronds rise to two or three feet, long and tapering, light green, thin and delicate, easily broken. From a distance, the foliage looks feathery and soft. The pinnae are lance-shaped and sharp-toothed, repeating in miniature the shape of the whole frond. The small, cup-shaped spore sacks form on the toothlets. The name of the fern comes from the fragrant wax carried in tiny, hair-covered glands; the odor is noticeable when you brush against the plant or bruise the fronds. The hay-scented fern is a beautiful yellow-green throughout the summer, but, sensitive to cold and early frost, it quickly withers away to light brown or bleaches to a pale wraith of its former self.

The SENSITIVE FERN (*Onoclea sensibilis*), renamed the BEAD FERN by Wherry in 1937, has very distinct sterile and fertile fronds. The sterile fronds are from one to two-and-a-half feet high, yellow-green, broadly triangular, and cut into oblong, wavy toothed sections; the lower pinnae almost reach to mid-vein, the upper are less deeply cut. The fruiting frond stands shorter and erect. The pinnules on this frond have rolled up into dark-green berrylike bodies or beads that enclose the spore cases, developing in June or July. The sensitive fern is not at all socially sensitive; it arrives brashly without invitation and spreads out. The new ferns encroach along the creeping root stock, which is hairy and tough, hard to oust from places where it isn't wanted. Like the hay-scented fern, this fern is easily affected by cold, and that sensitivity is probably what gave it its name, although the spore-bearing fronds dry to a dark brown and stand stiffly through the winter months into spring.

In contrast, the CHRISTMAS FERN (*Polystichum acrostichoides*) stays green all winter. The hardiness of the fern is reflected in its description: root stock stout, chaffy, stipe and rachis (mid-vein) very scaly, blade lancelate. The pinnae are narrow, somewhat pointed, shiny, dark green, and leathery. They contract toward the top of the frond, giving it a stylized evergreen shape, which may partly account for its name—that, and its use in Christmas decorations. The fruit dots form on the back of the fertile fronds in close, rough, brown patches. Parsons describes the young fronds as "curled up like tawny caterpillars." They appear in April among the old ones, which are still green but bowed to the ground with age.

1987

JANUARY 8

Today I found a rabbit hiding under a Christmas fern in the wildflower garden. As I was walking back toward the house, a raucous honking filled the sky and one ragged "V" of geese after another wheeled restlessly over my head. It was a gray sky, and although not cold, there was nothing in it of spring. A winter day, except for the rabbit.

1989

DECEMBER 13

After clearing the front path and driveway of last night's snowfall and carrying in the empty trash can—which, thank goodness, was not the one I heard the snowplow dump over in the dark at 6:30 A.M.—I brushed the snow off the boxwoods so they wouldn't break open with the weight. Then I went into the wild garden and followed the rabbit tracks around the paths. It was beautiful out there in the snow this bright morning, and peaceful.

Last Christmas, Rachel gave me a "crying rabbit" paperweight, "inspired by the delicately worked rabbits found in late medieval millefleurs (thousand flowers) tapestries." This rabbit is taken from one of the French tapestries, now in the Cluny Museum in Paris. Against a rose background embroidered with flowers and leaves, a small brown rabbit is sitting up on its haunches, with one paw held to its soft brown eye. No one seems to have interpreted the meaning of the rabbit's tears, but the series of the Lady and the Unicorn tapestries do tell a story, for in an age of symbolism like the Middle Ages, everything had an inner meaning.

Margaret Freeman, in *The Unicorn Tapestries*, her fine book on the "Hunt of the Unicorn" tapestries in the Cloisters in New York, has these paragraphs on the rabbits:

> The French *Ortus Sanitatis* states that rabbits "give birth many times a year," have "little ones without number," and "multiply marvelously." This not obscure characteristic is sufficient reason to include rabbits in a set of tapestries supposedly woven for a marriage. In the Middle Ages, when the uniting of two people in wedlock was expected to produce heirs who would carry on the family name and administer the estates, fertility was as important as chastity.
>
> Rabbits are conspicuous in all six of the Lady with the Unicorn tapestries in the Cluny Museum, which, as noted, may also have been designed to celebrate a wedding. They appear also in many medieval works of art, not necessarily because of their significance but because of their undeniable charm.
>
> **PAGE 80**

Significance of spring and fertility, as well as their "undeniable charm" and all the ties of affection to children's beloved stories, are more than enough reasons to have rabbits in the wildflower garden. Often, when I walk there, I will start a rabbit and be startled. Or sometimes I will spy the rabbit who thinks himself still hidden, tense among the greenery until he judges me just too close to bear and darts away. In the early summer, when I'm on my knees weeding, sometimes I'll push aside leaves and find a smooth hollow with a few soft hairs, the form where a rabbit has lain. Sadly, once in the wild garden I found a dead rabbit. I buried it under a puny evergreen, thinking that it might nourish the tree as the Native Americans buried a fish with the seed to help the maize grow.

Many of the snakeroot flowers had gone to gray,
bristle-tipped seeds that floated in the cool, bright air.

$\mathcal{S}$UMMER $\mathcal{W}$EEDING

JUNE/JULY/AUGUST

LOVE OF FLOWERS AND VEGETABLES IS NOT ENOUGH
TO MAKE A GOOD GARDENER. HE MUST ALSO HATE WEEDS.

EUGENE BERTIN

1997

MAY 22

It has been a beautiful spring! But now the dogwood petals, curled and a little brown, are caught along the edges of the path like rifts of old snow. It is evident that whatever the calendar says, spring is over and summer is "a-comin' in."

Spring is the hopeful season, because then all things seem possible. Nature hasn't gotten ahead of me yet, and there is potential for perfection in my lawn and garden. When we are at the spring of life, young and idealistic, and the bad things in our human nature haven't gotten ahead of us yet, then perfection does seem rather easily attainable. That's because our weeds are still lurking underground, except for that earliest of weeds, the WILD GARLIC *(Allium vincale)*.

The milk I drank as a child was set on the farmhouse doorstep in glass quart bottles by Eddie, the milkman. It came from the dairy farm that was back-to-back with apple trees on one side of the orchard. The cows, turned out to pasture in early spring, hungrily chomped up anything green, and with the green being mostly the garlic, the milk reeked and tasted of it for several weeks.

I call it wild garlic because my parents did, but other people call this blue-green, hollow-stemmed, pungent member of the lily family "onion grass," often with a curse. The tuft of leaves does come up from white bulbs that are more like onions than garlic cloves. Unlike the wild garlic pictured in the wildflower guides, this plant only grows about six inches high and doesn't flower or even come to a head in the lawn. But it is ragged and smelly, and it spoils the grass. As the ground softens after frost, I know that I should get out there and dig up the bulbs. That is the only way to get rid of them. But as I also do with my embedded imperfections, I wish the garlic would just go away without effort. I take the lazy way out and mow it short; then it blends in with the grass (an example of the cop-out that "what you don't see doesn't hurt you").

In springtime, with a beneficent eye (for everything but wild garlic), I let the tender plant and the tender weed grow up together like wheat and tares, because pulling out the weed may destroy the flower, too. Weeds aren't much to worry about for a while; so pass the months of April and May. Suddenly, it's June. In my corner of the world, June is a summer month, with a strong sun that builds heat and humidity, brings out full leaf on every tree, pushes the weeds up out of the earth a half a foot a day (or so it seems). There's no doubt then that it's time, in the summer of our maturity, to take action against the weeds, and already almost too late.

1987

JUNE 10

Somehow we slipped into June—the spring of expectations is behind us. There is so much growth! The early order brought about by my careful planting, clipping, and edging is gone in an explosion of greenery. The gardener is no longer in control, but fighting hard just to keep her head above the green tide.

Whoever said, "Summertime and the livin' is easy," didn't have a garden. Summer is hard, hot work for the gardener. One has to love the process of gardening as much as the product, maybe more, or it is a weary business. It can even be a dangerous one.

About ten years ago, deer ticks arrived in our area carrying Lyme disease (so named because it was first discovered in Lyme,

Connecticut, in 1980). Eastern Montgomery County is now thought to be the hot spot for Lyme in Pennsylvania, and I think Bryn Athyn may well be the center of the spot. So far, I have not gotten Lyme disease, but a great many people I know have. Some people have moved out of the more wooded areas of the borough because they were so weary of being reinfected. Ticks are more likely to be in brushy places, tall weeds, or long grass, but they feed off all kinds of wild creatures: rabbits, mice, and birds, not just deer. They cling to pets and people and may be carried onto lawns or into the house. Once I found one crawling on the back of the toilet tank in the downstairs powder room. When I pounded it dead with a hammer on the back doorstep it oozed blood. It had bitten something, animal or human—maybe me. The thought made my blood run cold.

The common dog tick is a nasty longtime resident, but this small newcomer is a real stinker, and its smallness does not make it cute. It is tiny—about the size of a coarsely ground black pepper grain—but ugly tough. This tick carries a spirochete bacterium that can make the large joints of the body swell, paralyze the face, or affect the heart. Lyme begins with symptoms that are similar to the flu: fever, aching, and extreme fatigue. Sometimes the victim gets the big, red bull's-eye around the bite and sometimes not. If not discovered in time and treated, the disease can cause permanent damage. It's a threat to be watched out for at any time of year, but especially in June and July, the peak time for the nymphs. I never go into the garden in high summer now without looking out for the little devils.

Although more messy than a menace, mulberries are a summer problem for me, too. The smell of rotting fruit combined with the nose tickle of blooming privet makes an unpleasant smell (at least it is a stench that I don't like). A big, old mulberry tree covers a lot of the wild garden. Hardly showing a leaf by the first of June, before you can turn around, it is dropping ripe, purple-black fruit, and the birds that feed on the juicy berries are dropping something else. Under the mulberry tree is not the place to be. When I come out to work before mid-July, I take my kneeling pad to the other end of the garden. And here I find plenty of weeding to do.

Fortunately, I have come to really like weeding, and I think it is good for me as well as the garden. After a frustrating day spent working on tedious tasks inside, I once wrote in my journal, "It would have been better for my health and my state of mind to have gotten out and pulled weeds."

"What is a weed?" asked the nineteenth-century American writer Ralph Waldo Emerson. And he answered himself: "A plant whose virtues have not yet been discovered." His definition, probably somewhat humorously intended, was echoed sentimentally by the poet James Russell Lowell:

> A weed is no more than a flower in disguise
> Which is seen through at once, if love give a man eyes.

Emerson believed that the value of a plant is in its virtue or use, an idea that he might have borrowed from Swedenborg, whom he had read fairly extensively. In his poem "To the Rhodora," Emerson follows this idea of virtue and use with another idea, that beauty is use, and "its own excuse for being." In his verse above, Lowell said, and rightly, I think, that what we see as beautiful is determined by what we love. The face of a beloved person is beautiful to us, and a plant that we cherish will always be a flower, even though it might seem a weed to someone else.

Originally the word *weed* was *we'od*, the Anglo-Saxon name for any herb or small plant. But the word underwent a pejorative shift over the centuries, and despite Emerson and Lowell and others, it is now defined in *Webster's Seventh New Collegiate Dictionary* as:

> A plant of no value and usually of rank growth; especially one
> that tends to overgrow or choke out more desirable plants.

In some circles, *weed* seems to have become an ugly word, like *evil*, because it implies a judgment. On a walk through the Pennypack Ecological Preservation Trust last year, I was amused to hear our guide call the porcelain berry vine, which is taking over and destroying the open woodlands, not a weed or even an alien, but an "exotic." Political correctness has caught up to the naturalists.

Some weeds fit Webster's description—plants of no value (no use). Some weeds go even further; they really are noxious. Charles Olds—who, as a doctor practicing general medicine in the early part of this century, must have seen cases of this poisoning—writes about the jimsonweed:

> [If, as I believe,] all plants are representative of man's spiritual state, thus representing something of either heaven or hell in him, we have a reason for the growth of weeds as well as of flowers . . . the Jimson-weed . . . is a loathsome plant. Coarse, repellent, malodorous, and with bat-like leaves, it thrives best amongst the rubbish of our back-door civilization. It loves garbage. And even its beautiful [white or purple trumpet-like] blossom, that might attract breathes forth the perfume of hell. No wonder it is poisonous. And it is violently so. Not to the touch like poison ivy or nettles, but from eating of it, especially of the seeds.
>
> Once you have seen a sure enough poisoning by the jimson-weed, you will not need to be told that there has been a slight opening of hell, and that at least one devil has escaped. . . . The delirium, the hallucinations, the fever. The excitement and furious raving over the terrible mental images that distress [the victim]. He sees animals, spirits, ghosts, devils (which, of course, is all part of the program). This is the mental picture. But other things are going on at the same time. And all put together result in either recovery or death. Much depending upon the prompt use of emetics, stomach-pumps, and other medical artillery.

This weed that bears the seed of madness and death does seem to be intimately connected with evil. But why? Without spiritual life, a plant is not of itself either good or evil. But it can represent, as Olds says, a spiritual state in human beings. In the beginning, all the plants created by God were useful and beautiful. Then we remember the curse laid on Adam because he abused the fruit of the tree of knowledge and chose his own way above Jehovah's:

> Cursed is the ground for your sake;
> In toil you shall eat of it

All the days of your life.
Both thorns and thistles it shall bring forth for you,
And you shall eat the herb of the field.

GENESIS 3: 17–18

Before Adam's sin against God, thorns and thistles and jimson-weed just weren't there.

To follow the words of Scripture with the jocular quotation from Rudyard Kipling below may seem profane, but the rhyme holds a pertinent truth, too, I think.

> Oh, Adam was a gardener, and God who made him sees
> That half a proper gardener's work is done upon his knees.

From this position of humility, on my knees in an attitude of prayer, I attack the physical weeds and the weeds in my spiritual garden, too. There is an obvious analogy between digging up harmful plants and weeding out poisonous thoughts, hurtful feelings, and bad actions. Weeding is like reformation. The only way to get rid of something that you don't want in yourself is to pull it out, dig it up, dispose of it. Sometimes this is hard and painful work. And we couldn't do it at all without prayer. Even so, it takes time, and often, despite the best efforts, a nasty weed or nasty inclination comes back. Just when I think I've gotten rid of that one at last, there it is springing up again in another place. The most tenacious are the ones that bring their own sweet delight, say, a honeysuckle vine; those bad habits we most enjoy are the ones we seem to have the greatest trouble weeding out.

Sometimes it is as difficult to separate the weeds from the flowers in our minds as in the garden. There are some fast-spreading and tenacious wildflowers threatening to take over my garden that I do not call weeds. Wherry in his *Wildflower Guide* says many of the wildflowers of other lands have made themselves at home here, and some are "so aggressive as to be classed as weeds—plants which crowd out more desirable ones." (Is it the characteristic of aggression that turns an acceptable or lovely plant or person into a weed?) It is true that the "more desirable" plants often are the weaker and more delicate; they are like those good affections, implanted in us from babyhood, that can so easily be crowded out by growing selfishness. These fragile, innocent flowers I must protect and cherish. But I don't want to get rid of the others completely either; in truth I doubt if I could now without plowing up the whole garden. My struggle is for containment, moderation, and proportion, for in the right place and in the right amount some pleasant "weeds" like earthly pursuits and pleasures can be delightful and even appropriate.

I find the hardest flower/weed to contain is the lesser celandine. Planting it carefully only where it's wanted is not a solution; it doesn't stay there. It spreads by seeds and by little nodules that break off in the ground. Sometimes I feel quite savage about the celandine and claw it out by the handfuls. Even if I pull it up by the roots or dig it out with a shovel, the nodules stay behind in the soil, and next spring, like spontaneous generation, there is the celandine, the same as ever, brisk and bright. It clogs the paths and threatens the Dutchman's-breeches and the bloodroots. It pops up under the Epimedium and roots itself in the heart of the Christmas fern. Trying to stop this spring tide is like King Canute commanding the waves to cease. However, like high tide, it does ebb, leaving by summer only a brown tracery like spent foam on the sand.

Another low-growing "pretty weed" I first saw in the Fromuth nursery is now in my wild garden, too. (It may have grown from the clump that Thane brought home all those years ago.) This plant has established itself in the stony strip this side of the fence between Homer's property and mine. As long as it behaves itself, I don't mind having it. Mrs. Fromuth did not have a name for the "weed" but after a little research I think this is either DOWNY or HAIRY WOOD MINT. It has the square stem that places it in the mint family. The blossoms are like those of self-heal or bugle (also mints), but more pink. However, the distinguishing characteristic is the many soft, furry leaves and bracts from among which the tiny flowers shyly peep.

There is nothing shy about JACK-BY-THE-HEDGE, as the British call it, or GARLIC MUSTARD (*Alliaria officinalis*) of the Cruciferae or cress family. When crushed by a trowel or gardening glove, the leaves give off a strong smell like garlic. It is one of the aliens that Wherry calls a weed. I think that I do, too. Although I allow a few of these plants to grow here and there, I pull most of them out. The leaves are more or less heart-shaped with rounded teeth at the edges, and if the winter is mild they stay green throughout. The stalk may rise as many as two feet, but sometimes it grovels. The flowers are white, four petals arranged crosswise, numerous, but not showy, in branching groups. The plant blooms from May through June with the seedpods of spent flowers forming while others are still budding. The pods are about an inch-and-a-half long, slightly curved, like little string beans.

INDIAN STRAWBERRY (in the rose family) is an alien that seems to grow all over my property, although it is supposed to prefer moist waste ground. It looks like a little yellow-flowered strawberry plant; the berry is red, very seedy, and inedible. Because of its crawling and tenacious habit, I tend to pull it out as if it was a weed, but actually, it is rather pretty.

Another plant that came to us originally from somewhere else and so is flourishing, as aliens do, is the low-growing GROUND IVY or GILL-OVER-THE-GROUND (*Glechoma hederacea*), another member of the square-stemmed mint family. It has small, scalloped, round leaves that stay a greenish-purple color through the fall and into the winter. In its long flowering period from April to July, the little violet-blue petals are very dainty. Is gill-over- the-ground really a weed? It is a weed in its manner of growth, but if I look at it with the eyes of love as Lowell suggests, it is a flower—a wildflower, anyway. I do try to weed it out of the gardens by the house where the soil is loose, because there are plenty of big ingrown patches that I can't separate from the sod in the lawn. But I think at least a bit of it deserves to be in the wild garden, too.

Out of interest, I looked ground ivy up in Gerard's herbal, and this is what he wrote about the plant in sixteenth-century England:

Ground Ivy is a low or base herbe; it creepeth and spreads upon the ground hither and thither all about, with many stalkes of an uncertaine length, slender, and like those of the Vine: whereupon grow leaves something board and round: amongst which come forth the floures gaping like little hoods, not unlike those of Germander of a purplish blew colour: the whole plant is of a strong smell and bitter taste.

. . . It is called in English Ground-Ivy, Ale-hoofe, Gill go by ground, Tune-hoof, and Cats-foot.

Ground-Ivy, Celendine, and Daisies, of each a like quantitie, stamped and strained, and a little sugar and rose water put thereto, and dropped with a feather into the eies, taketh away all manner of inflammation, spots webs, itch, smarting, or any griefe whatsoever in the eyes. . . . The women of our Northerne parts . . . do turne the herbe Ale-hoofe into their Ale; but the reason thereof I know not.

This plant, by Emerson's definition, is not a weed because it has, or at least had, its practical uses. In the season of its blooming, it is also pretty, and thus useful for beauty's sake. But as Charles Olds says:

There are some weeds that are weeds, and their very names stamp them as weeds. Such are pokeweed, chickweed, bindweed, milkweed, and many others. Of course they are not all *herba inutilis [useless plants]* by any means. But they are more or less noxious, troublesome, or have some other civilized taint adhering to them that makes them not wanted, unnecessary in the perfect garden. Not that there is any such perfection this side of Heaven. But we nevertheless seek it. And we all know how to remove weeds and warts. . . . just now I am after the pokeweed.

POKEWEED (*Phytolacca americana*) is the only member of the pokeweed family listed in either Peterson or Wherry. I am grateful to these authors for being broad-minded enough to list some weeds among their wildflowers, otherwise how could we learn about them? And I have enjoyed learning about them even if I don't particularly want them in my garden. I'm not quite sure whether I want the pokeweed or not. Wherry calls it "weedy, and worth growing only for bird food." The birds do love the fruit. One plant for interest and the birds' sake might be all right.

The trouble is that pokeweed always seems to come up and flourish just in the wrong spot. The coarse, woody plant with large kalelike leaves takes up a lot of room. A two-year-old plant can stand four to five feet high. That is a formidable height for anything in a small garden, especially something in the wrong place. And usually the pokeweed does not stand alone; like Hamlet's foes it comes not as single spies, but in battalions. For each plant bears a lot of purple-black berries on red stalks, and a lot of the berries become next year's plants. It is self-aggrandizing. On principle, this selfish attitude is definitely one to keep in check.

They say that the leaves of the pokeweed can be boiled and eaten like spinach. I have not been tempted to try them. The berries, gourmet food for birds, are poisonous for humans, but I was never tempted to try them, either. When I was young, I used to squeeze the ripe berries and use the juice as ink, with a pigeon feather as a quill pen. But my son was a far more adventurous child than I was, and I was nervous about introducing pokeberry ink to my children for fear that Thane would drink it. He once saw cardinals eating yew berries and gave them a try himself. We waited for him to sicken, but he didn't. So perhaps some of these alarums are unfounded. The root of the pokeweed is also supposed to be poisonous. It is thick and tapers to a long point; when one tries to dig it up and slices it with a spade, it cracks and splits like a raw sweet potato. Like a potato, even a small piece of root will make a new plant. If I discard a pokeweed root behind the garden shed or on the compost pile, it turns itself around, digs in, and starts afresh.

The weeds that I really hate seem to be completely useless and even vicious, for they throttle the life out of other plants and trees: the murderers. Among the worst are poison ivy and wild grape.

It's hard to imagine that POISON IVY was once imported into England as a ground cover. Those people must have gotten a nasty surprise. The plant is handsome enough, with three glossy, irregularly notched lobes to a leaf, rich green in the summer and flaming with color in the autumn. But not content to eat the dust of the ground, like a hairy serpent it climbs up the trunks of trees and hangs in the branches. From the vantage of height it broadcasts its seeds or sends them off in the bellies of birds disguised as blue-white berries to propagate where they evacuate. Besides strangling trees, the ivy has a poison that infects people, biting the hand that touches it. The venom can cause a fiery itch, a red rash that crawls over the skin, and in acute cases, it swells the tissues. For some, the plant is so lethal that they don't even need to touch it. A breeze blowing off the leaves or smoke from a fire burning dead vines can cause a reaction. Fortunately, I inherited my father's immunity and not my mother's susceptibility, but I treat the plant with caution even so. If I inadvertently brush against it when out walking, I go home, wash my skin with brown soap, and put my clothes in the laundry. When I find it in the garden, I wear gloves to pull it up and put it in a trash bag, never in the compost pile. The trick is to stop it before it has a chance to become entrenched and work its woe. Sometimes I think of this poisonous plant as representative of malicious gossip—the kind of wicked talk that kills a person's good name and reputation if it spreads around, and can destroy his or her useful life in society.

Another serial killer of trees and shrubs is the Wild Grape or Porcelain Berry, but this does not carry a personal poison. I'm sure that I heard from someone who tried them that the small, bright blue-green globes are edible, but very bitter—the origin of "sour grapes," perhaps. Wild grape comes up all over my garden every year. Some are shoots from well-rooted vines—a thumb width thick or more—that run along the ground, drop a root anchor every now and again, and send up a flare of leaves. These vines are old-timers; they resist cutting and won't be dug out. They reach up, sometimes two feet or more, with groping tendrils to catch the low branches of a tree or shrub and begin to climb. In a short time, they reach the top and spread a shroud of leaves over the branches. Along a neglected roadside or in the open woods around us, we see where the green tenants have killed the host and brought its house to the ground. To prevent this from happening in my garden, I pull the vines down and hack away at their roots. But there are also the seedlings. Pulling these is like having a salamander by the tail; the brittle top stalk breaks off and leaves an inch of hard-to-see earth-brown stem and the root behind. If left for dead, the plant rejuvenates in less than a week and is off and running. I wonder if one might think of wild grape as a smothering kind of love that kills off another person's initiative and freedom to grow. It bears fruit, but the fruit is bitter.

A vine that works more slowly and graciously, but will eventually rot out a tree, is ENGLISH IVY. Perhaps one might see the traditional ivy as the encirclement of convention. The ivy was there before my garden, and the festoons of dark greenery smooth away the stark outlines of winter in the trees and add an established and old-world air to the upstart Norway maple and mulberry. My neighbor and I have both let it creep up the trees that straddle our joint property line at the back of the garden. Now with the fence built around them, half of the ivy is on his side and half on mine. In a fit of zealous preservation, I could try to clear the half that protrudes into my garden, but I doubt if he would bother about his half, so what would be the gain? Besides, sometimes one has to compromise, even with faults.

Other vines in the garden are woodbine, which grows over the stump of a chokecherry tree, and an abandoned wisteria that never blooms, from someone's arbor in days past. I rather like the woodbine. It turns a deep red in the autumn.

Among other weeds that aren't social climbers—that stay on the ground—are some whose names I don't know. There is a fleshy weed with pale yellow-green, almost translucent stems and little seeds like sand grains that hang onto the cutwork leaves. There is a weed with a bad odor, whose leaves look like those of a chrysanthemum, but it doesn't flower, or I've never seen it do so. I think I have eradicated that one. Then there is one I'm determined to eradicate that loves to hide under the mayapples as if they were a tax shelter.

After the mayapples fruit and die back, it gets its day in the sun. Each branching stem is covered with tiny burrs that ripen and dry and hang on all winter if nothing comes along to carry them off, yet drop at the slightest tremor if you try to pull up the mother plant.

My weeding is usually a solitary occupation. But sometimes it's a pleasure to work with a group, somewhere other than in my own garden. About four or five years ago, an enterprising young woman in our community started her own business in designing and planting perennial gardens. She volunteered to enliven the gardens around the Bryn Athyn Cathedral, which had become rather static, alternating between tulips in the spring and annuals in the summer, turning them into fragrant and delightful panoramas of blooms throughout the seasons. To help with the maintenance of the extensive gardens, Danielle began a volunteer group she named the Weed Patrol, which met on Saturday mornings. For a while I was a fairly regular member of this group, which ranged from six to twenty, who love gardening and the church. The Weed Patrol didn't meet if it rained or snowed, but I've been out there in some chill winds in early spring and some sweaty, not-a-leaf-stirring mornings in the summer. But companionship in pulling weeds or deadheading makes the hour pass quickly, and sharing the satisfaction of the work is good for the soul.

1996

AUGUST 4

If we'd get some really cool, clear weather I'd be tempted into the wildflower garden to weed (imagine being tempted to weed). But because of all the rain and humidity, everything is so sodden and sour out there now, and probably so tick infested, that I don't even like walking through. Leaves from the Norway maple at the edge of the garden are dying on the tree, falling from the branches and littering the lawn like bits of charred paper. Soon the tree will die altogether, and I'll have to have it taken down. My whole world seems rather dead-end right now. Perhaps I'll go and weed at the church this morning; I feel a need to get in touch with a garden.

The big Norway maple at the front edge of the wildflower garden did die and had to be cut down. The next summer, the absence of the big tree opened up the sky at that end of the garden and let in a lot more sunlight. With sun and air came a stampede of all kinds of wild growth. First, the dame's rocket took off like a rocket, and a languishing buttercup filled its cup with sunshine. A couple of stalks of goldenrod went seven feet tall and collapsed on top of the forsythia. The orange daylilies that had been languishing in the shade bloomed joyfully. The hitherto modest DAYFLOWER (*Commelina communis*) quite forgot itself, sprawling all over in an unseemly fashion. In my ignorance, I used to call this plant cornflower because the leaves were the shape of the leaves on sweet corn, although not so large and rough. Now I know that a cornflower is quite another thing altogether. The dayflower blossom is a simple one, with two upper bright blue petals and a very small lower one that is whitish. The branching stems, with joints like elbows, do look like spider's legs and identify the plant as a member of the spiderwort family. These fleshy stems are brittle and break off with a snap when one tries to pull the plant up by the root.

But the flower/weed that really had a heyday was the WHITE SNAKEROOT. Until last year, it was content to stay in the background until it rose to its customary height of two feet and brought out its fuzzy, white blossoms in late summer, glimmering here and there among the leafy shadows. But in the newly bright end of the garden, by mid-August, it had grown into a three- to four-foot hedge of soft, rather heart-shaped leaves, branching stems, and flat-topped bloom clusters. In keeping with the family name thoroughwort, it had thoroughly taken over, completely blocking the path. It just goes to show what can happen when a plant can bask in the sunshine. And this is true of people, too; when they are no longer love-deprived, they blossom forth all over the place.

I let the snakeroot go while it was looking so lush and attractive, but by the end of September, I was beginning to think about order and sparseness, and so waded in to the jungle with clippers and a spade. Many of the flowers were gone to gray, bristle-tipped seeds that floated in the cool, bright air of a perfect early-autumn day and made me sneeze. The stalks were tough, and I had to go to the garden shed for the loppers to cut some of the thickest. The roots were even tougher. I dug them out if I could and left the others, hoping that winter would make them more amenable to removal. The root doesn't look anything like a snake, being a bunch of white stringlike tentacles that spread around the main stalk in a fibrous pad. The root isn't venomous, either, although the leaves have a poison, Wherry tells me, which if eaten by cows gets into their milk and can make people sick. There are no cows in my yard to make bad milk by eating snakeroot leaves, but I heed the warning, for other kinds of weeds can get in my spiritual system and make me sick to death.

> As with the heart, so with the garden, if any spot . . . is left untilled up springs an evil weed. . . . Let us plant with diligence and care the garden of the soil, but let us, with far deeper earnestness tend the garden of our hearts.
>
> **THE COTTAGE GARDENER, 1849**

When I was younger and had more family to care for and a tighter schedule, I used to allot different jobs to different days of the week—Sunday was my day for working in the garden. A very fitting day, if one thinks of the garden of the heart as well as the garden of the soil, and of pulling weeds as getting rid of evil things in oneself.

One afternoon when he came to work for me, I asked my grandson Adam if he liked working in the garden. His answer was noncommittal. "Its all right. You sort of get in stride with it."

I know what he means—getting in stride is what keeps me working at a hard job long after I'm tired. I want the satisfaction of seeing the job done: the pruned tree, the weeded garden, the smooth lawn, more than I want to rest. But Adam doesn't yet seem to be into the deeper satisfaction of gardening that restores the spirit. Maybe that has to wait until you are working on your own garden and on the secret garden of your soul.

A truly beautiful garden, the external and the internal, is the Lord's doing—nothing would grow without his heat and light, his love and wisdom. I realize that I only serve as an undergardener. So, humbly, I tend my natural garden, and I try to work at the same time on what needs attention in my spiritual garden: pulling out that nasty thought about my neighbor, cutting back a bad habit, nurturing and feeding that tender affection for truth, trimming away the tangled growth of woody self-intelligence, and all the time thanking God for the beauty of his creation and the daily strength he gives me to bring fulfillment to my life.

Dogwood seedlings, as well as other curious species,
were brought to Swedenborg from the New World.

SWEDENBORG'S HEAVENLY GARDENS

MAN IS BOTH THE GARDEN AND THE GARDENER.
ANDERS HALLENGREN

We take up gardening, I believe, at a turning point in our lives. Our interest in a new and meaningful activity comes when we feel ready for a new approach to life. For me, the right moment came when my children were old enough to manage on their own for an hour or two. For others, it may come when their children are grown, when they change jobs, or when they retire from a demanding career. The tranquil hours we spend in the garden give us an opportunity to be intimately in touch with God's creation, to reflect on and nurture the inner life of our being. It is then that a person becomes both a natural and spiritual gardener.

For one man particularly, this was most profoundly true. Emanuel Swedenborg, a prominent scientist and inventor in eighteenth-century Sweden, had led a most productive life; he was a practical man of affairs as well as a scholar and a writer of many scientific and philosophical books. After his family was ennobled, he took his seat in the Swedish House of Nobles and became involved with the workings of the government. He held a position as an assessor on the important Board of Mines, which controlled much of the considerable mineral wealth of the country. Swedenborg might almost have been called the prototype of the man of the Age of Enlightenment. And then, in his middle fifties, several great changes took place in his life, and one of them was that he took up gardening.

For many years, Swedenborg had lived in rented lodgings. But although he was a single gentleman without pretensions, he apparently felt that now he wanted his own home, a comfortable, pleasant place to live, and space where he could read, meditate, and write for long periods without disturbance. In 1743, he bought a large property on Hornsgatan, a street that ran through the Sodermalm section of the city of Stockholm. Here he planned to build a modest house and surround it with a beautiful garden. In March, just before he went to Holland on another of his extended trips to publish his manuscripts, a gardener was engaged to live on the property and to oversee general improvements while the master was away.

It was during the next two years that Swedenborg reached a crucial point in his life and changed the focus of his writing, turning from scientific studies and a search for the seat of the soul in the natural body to intense concentration on the Word of God. While abroad, Swedenborg composed a comprehensive Bible index and wrote and published Parts I and II of a small work titled the *Worship and Love of God*. He also kept a journal of his dreams, which were often tumultuous and had the effect of initiating him into a deep concern for things beyond the natural world. Before he returned to Sweden, he had answered a divine call to experience, write down, and publish matters of great spiritual significance. From this time until his death in 1772, he was able to live fully and consciously in two worlds, often simultaneously. It was to begin this new mission that he took up residence at number 43 Hornsgatan in the summer of 1745.

The following quotation from *Heaven and Hell*, paragraph 489:4, one of his early theological books, might almost have been written about himself:

> Those who have loved science and have thereby cultivated
> their rational faculty and acquired intelligence, and at the
> same time have acknowledged the Divine—these in the other
> life have their pleasure in knowledge, and their rational de-
> light changed into spiritual delight, which is delight in know-
> ing good and truth. They dwell in gardens where flower beds
> and grass plots are beautifully arranged, with rows of trees

round about, and arbors and walks, the trees and flowers
changing from day to day. The entire view imparts delight to
their minds in a general way, and the variations in detail continually renew the delight.

Swedenborg found that "in the other life" people lived in homes
and gardens that imaged the things they knew and loved. The more
wise and loving the dwellers, the more beautiful their surroundings.
Their environment was, as it were, created from the inside out. And
I think we can see an approximation of that here on earth, too, although the material restrictions of this world are limiting. We can
often tell by the decoration of a house or the way a garden is planted
and cared for what kind of a person lives there. Our own garden can
reflect our inner life.

When Swedenborg came home to Stockholm, he had the opportunity to lay out a garden that would express what he was, the
things he knew and loved, and the activities that he wanted to engage in. He explains in *True Christian Religion,* paragraph 336, that

> In the laying out of a garden, the first thing . . . is to level the
> ground, prepare the soil, and plant trees in it and sow the
> seeds of such things as will be of use, while the first . . .
> [intention] is the use of its products. . . . Does not everyone
> who wishes to build a temple or a house, or to lay out a
> garden, or cultivate a field first intend some use? And does he
> not continually keep this in mind and meditate upon it while
> he is procuring the means to it?

From this passage one surmises that the intention or purpose of
Swedenborg's own garden was its various uses—not just the practical and external use of growing flowers, herbs, vegetables, and
fruits that benefitted the body, but the spiritual and internal uses
that benefitted the mind. From all of this resulted the garden's
beauty and delight.

We know something of the way in which Swedenborg laid out
his physical garden from descriptions by F. G. Lindh in a piece titled
"Swedenborg, a Resident of Sodermalm," and from an article

signed J. C. L. S. that appeared in *The Intellectual Repository*, published in London, 1867. At least one of these written observations came after the heyday of the garden, but from these accounts two diagrams were drawn that help us to see what Swedenborg's property looked like more than two hundred years ago. They show a garden that drew on the traditional order and balance characteristic of this historical time period, and reflected the restrictions of a northern climate. But they also demonstrate Swedenborg's own predilections. His curiosity and scientific bent of mind were satisfied in an orangery, or area for experimentation with new species; his growing knowledge of the correspondences of trees and flowers to spiritual things showed itself in the variety of plants he cultivated; his sociability and interest in people can be seen in the structures he had built in the garden to give enjoyment to his visitors.

From these descriptions and drawings, I picture Swedenborg's garden in my imagination as it might have looked at its height. Around the house were narrow beds with flowers to delight the eye and herbs for the kitchen. There was a shrubbery close by with box bushes clipped into shapes: geometrical forms, birds, and animals. Lime trees grew in a line along the fence that divided the house and open courtyard from the main gardens. These extensive gardens were entered formally through a tall carved arch or gateway still in place, ninety-some years after Swedenborg's death, as described by J. C. L. S.

The gardens were laid out in a square divided into quadrants by walks crossing in the middle. At the point where the dissecting paths met was a small garden house or gazebo of trellis work, copied after a pavilion that Swedenborg had seen in a garden in England. From here the central walkway led on to the eastern end of the garden, where the summerhouse stood. Each quadrant was variously planted. In one area nearest to the house, stately trees graced a lawn interspersed with flowerbeds. Across the central walk was a big vegetable garden for the use of the household; the gardener was entitled to sell the surplus. A third section was given over to the orchard of fruit trees that could withstand a Swedish winter: apples, pears, and cherries. In the corner of the garden furthest from the street was a maze, typical of pleasure gardens of the time, an intricate design of interlocking hedges in which it was possible to be lost for hours (we are told).

Visitors to the garden could sit comfortably in the pavilion on a warm summer afternoon and hold a pleasant conversation, or continue their stroll by taking the path to the left, which led to a large voliere, or birdhouse, filled with doves and singing birds set in a rosebed. The aviary may have been added because of a dream of Swedenborg's, which was recorded in his diary for February 16, 1749:

> I have sometimes observed in sleep that in my garden at
> Stockholm there were various dovecotes (mansions of doves)
> near the earth with stone entrances, enclosures and chambers
> of beautiful construction. I wondered that there were such
> things in my garden and yet I had not known it.

It seems from this account that in early 1749, Swedenborg did not have a birdhouse in his garden, for he wonders to find one there in his dream. He knew, though, that the birds of the heavens correspond to the affection for spiritual truths, so it would be right to find them in a garden that represents the human mind. He wrote in *Arcana Coelestia*, "When angels are talking about knowledges, ideas, and influx, there appear . . . birds formed according to the subject of their conversation" (paragraph 3219).

Even on our natural level of expression, we speak of the dove of peace, and pairs of doves are symbols of marriage love. In the garden, when a brightly colored cardinal flashes by like a bright idea, it is a moment of delight. The songs of birds in springtime lift our hearts. Think how happy the children who came to visit must have been to discover the birds in Swedenborg's garden.

If the visitors took the right-hand path from the latticed pavilion, they would come to what appeared to be a gate through the high wooden wall into the Hornsgatan. But when the doors were opened, instead of the street, they found a mirror in which the whole garden in its variety was reflected. As Swedenborg wrote in *Heaven and Hell,* paragraph 56

> [V]ariety gives delight; and the nature of variety, as is known, is what determines the delight. From all this, it can be seen as in a mirror how perfection comes from variety even in heaven. For the things that exist in the natural world reflect the things of the spiritual world.

Swedenborg, in several other places, writes of the interior of things being seen through the exterior as an image is presented in a mirror. It fascinates me that this mirror in the garden was hung behind a door that looked like a gate, symbolic of entrance into understanding about another world.

There is an anecdote recounted about this mirror and a little girl named Greta Askbom. Swedenborg, unmarried and childless, nevertheless loved children, and they were attracted to him because of his gentle kindness. Once, when Greta came to visit, she asked Herr Swedenborg if he would please show her an angel, because she had heard grownups talk about how he often saw and talked to them. In his usual courteous manner, but probably with a twinkle in his eye, Swedenborg promised to show her an angel. He led her through his garden to what seemed to be a gate in the high fence. Opening the doors on the mirror, he showed the little girl herself, standing in the reflected garden, like an angel-child. What a charming way for Greta to learn that angels are real people who have lived at one time on this earth.

There is a passage in Swedenborg's *Divine Love and Wisdom,* paragraph 63, that reminds me of this incident:

> [T]here is a relation of all things of the created universe to humankind. . . . [I]n the spiritual world this is seen clearly. In that world, there are spirits of the three [heavenly] kingdoms, and in the midst of them an angel; he sees them around him, and also knows that they are representations of himself; yes, when the deepest part of his understanding is opened, he rec-

ognizes himself in the others, and sees his image in them, . . .
as in a mirror.

To the casual visitor, this garden might have looked like other
European gardens of the time. On his journeys, Swedenborg would
have had an opportunity to visit many such carefully planned and
geometric gardens. All this system and structure went along with
the prevalent philosophical idea of God as the one who had set up
the natural laws of physics. He was the technician of the universe.
With the expertise of a skilled mechanic, he fitted all the parts of the
world together like a watch, wound it up, and set it spinning. Then,
he withdrew with a benign smile to observe from afar while humans
tried to figure it all out. In the eighteenth century, it was thought
that science and rationality were the keys to unlocking the master
plan, and reason became a kind of religion.

Swedenborg was a rational man who loved the sciences and had
spent more than half of his lifetime trying to figure out how the natural world worked, but he was beginning to gain a different idea of
God based on his spiritual experiences. He saw, behind the orderly
structure of creation, a new concept of a creator who loved what he
had made and was continually present in its operation. Not a distant clock maker, but a God who "performs all the workings of nature by means of the spiritual world," as he relates in *True Christian
Religion*, paragraph 12:9.

Although it was not in the middle of the garden, perhaps the
true focus of Swedenborg's garden was his summerhouse. The original building, much the same as it is described below, is now in the
Skansen outdoor museum in Sweden.

> At the end of the walk are two poplars; behind them is the
> summer-house, which looks down the garden walk between
> the trees. It occupies the middle of the end of the garden and
> is about fourteen feet square. There are three stone steps up to
> the door sill, a double door, on each side a window [with
> shutters]; a vine gathers over them and the top of the door
> and clambers partly over the roof. . . .

Like the [main] house, the summer-house is built of logs [cov-
ered with boards], raised on a granite foundation about a couple of feet from the ground. It is as gay in color as the house—
dark red lines on yellow ground, with white window frames
and a black roof. . . . The roof does not go up to a ridge or
gable but is broken through by a short vertical portion, in
which are long narrow windows serving to light the loft over
the room. This, in turn, is roofed with hip rafters. On the two
points of this ridge is a ball ornament, on which is perched a
little gold star.

J. C. L. S., 1867

Swedenborg fitted out the summerhouse as a sort of
warm-weather study, and it was here, looking out on the beauties of
his garden, that he planned to work long hours writing his theological books inspired by the Lord.

Throughout all his theological works, there are many references
to gardens, seeds, flowers, and trees and the spiritual things they
represent. But the biggest clustering of these references comes in
the *Arcana Coelestia*, which was the first of Swedenborg's theological writings. The *Arcana* is an explication of Genesis and Exodus,
and the first volume examines the Creation and the Garden of Eden.
This would seem to have been an especially appropriate volume to
have written at home in his own garden, but in June of 1747,
Swedenborg again went abroad. He was not to return again until
the spring of 1750, bringing with him seeds from Europe, to at-
tempt germination.

The *Arcana* was begun in France in the winter of 1748-1749.
That Swedenborg was often troubled during this time about things
at home as well as other matters is reflected in this passage in his
Spiritual Diary, dated October 21, 1748:

As often as it was given me to think of my garden, of him who
had the care of it, of my being called home, of money matters,
of the state of mind of those that were known to me, or the
state or character of those in my house, of things that I was to
write, especially how they would be received by others, and the
possibility that they would not be understood, of new

garments that were to be obtained and various other things of this kind—whenever I was held for sometime in this kind of reflection the spirits would throw in inconvenient, troublesome and evil suggestions—when I had no thought about [these concerns] for sometime I had no care about them and no trouble.

It must have been difficult for him to give over the care of his newly made home and garden and go abroad again after only two years in Sweden—hard for a man who was used to being in control of his own life to put aside all worry over material matters and trust completely in the Lord. It reminds me of the Scripture passage that urges us to take no thought for the things of the body, but to seek first the Kingdom of Heaven. When Swedenborg followed this injunction he was in a state of peace, free of disorderly thoughts and frustrations. It is interesting that the following passage from the *Arcana*, paragraph 99, seems to follow directly from the *Spiritual Diary* entry above, and may have been written about the same time.

> When people are in order, they are called the Garden in Eden from the East, for they are then in the Lord's kingdom, or living a life as God would have them live. . . . Their state at this point enables them to be with angels in heaven, and to be virtually one among them. In fact, humanity has been so created that, while living on earth, people may be at the same time in heaven. In that situation, all of a person's thoughts . . . and even words or deeds lie open, containing what is celestial and spiritual.

When I read these words, a picture comes to my mind of a garden lying open to the sun and the rain. When we are in a state of spiritual order, we are like a garden that lies "open all the way from the Lord." Perhaps this is why we so often feel happy and at peace in a garden. "The pleasure of the affections of good must be likened to the delights the mind takes in gardens and flower-beds" (*Divine Providence*, paragraph 40). In describing the gardens in heaven, Swedenborg wrote, "The pleasant and beautiful things of these paradises are not what affect the beholder, but the celestial spiritual things that live in them" (*Arcana Coelestia*, paragraph 1588). Because we, too, may be in a heavenly state and at the same time living on earth, I think that we can experience something of those inner beauties in looking at natural gardens even as Swedenborg did.

Let us imagine how Swedenborg might have passed a summer's day when he was at home:

> Awaking once soon after daybreak, I went out into the garden in front of my house, and saw the sun rising in his glory, and round about him a halo, at first faint, but afterwards more distinct, and beaming like gold; and beneath its border was a rising cloud, which from the sun's rays glowed like a ruby. It set me thinking about the fables of the most ancient people which depicted Aurora with wings of silver and countenance of gold.
>
> With my mind immersed in the delights of these meditations, I came into the spirit.

TRUE CHRISTIAN RELIGION, PARAGRAPH 112

Then, as he sat in his summerhouse and wrote on into the morning, the garden before him would have been a wonderful source of metaphor and example. For "the herb-bearing seed is every truth which regards use, and the tree . . . [with fruit] is the good of faith" (*Arcana Coelestia*, paragraph 57).

Perhaps around noon, Swedenborg would lay down his pen and take a refreshing stroll along the paths of his garden, and then an analogy would come to him:

> When people enter the next life and bring with them the truths of faith in the spiritual memory, they seem to themselves to walk among cultivated hills, and also in gardens. . . . [T]he things which are of life are represented in heaven by gardens, olive groves, vineyards, and by flower beds and shrubberies.

ARCANA COELESTIA, PARAGRAPH 9841

In the pleasant evenings after his work, he may have opened the double doors of the summerhouse to the fragrant air and sat down to play at his little gold and white chamber organ. One can imagine the music drifting out among the trees.

When it got too cold to write in the summerhouse or work in the garden, Swedenborg would have had to move indoors. On the ground floor of his simple wooden house were three rooms: a front room for receiving visitors, a study for writing in the middle, and a small room at the end for sleeping. Upstairs was a large open area with a skylight facing south and a brick floor; this was probably used as a greenhouse. Perhaps there was also another chamber, for J. C. L. S. mentions that there was a dormer window piercing the roof "so as to look fairly through the lime trees, exactly opposite the garden gate and the distant summer-house." In the winter months, the summerhouse must have seemed very distant indeed, and the garden would have been blanketed by snow, but Swedenborg's botanical interests could have been carried on. Perhaps he had flats of sprouting seeds upstairs in the improvised greenhouse that would grow to plants in time for setting out in the spring.

It was in the eighteenth century that the science of botany really began. Carl Linnaeus, a contemporary of Swedenborg and a cousin by marriage, is credited with being the founder of this organic science. He was a keen botanist who set out to systematically classify all the plants in the known world. Linnaeus led parties of students into the fields and forests of Sweden to collect samples, and he encouraged the more adventuresome to take ship and explore known and unknown lands for new species. He divided plants into twenty-four categories according to their sexual characteristics, and he labeled them with Latin names that gave their genus and species. This once-innovative system is still in use today, although many more plants and subclassifications have been added to the original list as more varieties have been discovered in remote places of the world. Also, plants do not follow undeviating laws, and no two living things are exactly alike; over time and location they change their characteristics and seem similar, but different, as I have discovered in trying to positively identify some of the plants in my wildflower garden.

Inspired by Linnaeus, many men and women of rank and leisure all over the world took up the hobby of horticulture and found delight in a firsthand acquaintance with plants, their habits and habitats. I wonder if Swedenborg was thinking of Linnaeus and other naturalists and horticulturists, and even of himself, when he wrote this entry in his journal, dated February 14, 1748: "To devote the mind to natural experience or science, such as horticulture and the like, does not prevent the reception of spiritual knowledges—they can be perfected after death".

Swedenborg was once talking with some newcomers to the other life, and he asked them what "learning about God and nature they brought with them from the world." This encounter is recorded in *True Christian Religion,* paragraph 12:1–2:

> "... [T]hey said. "Nature is the operative power in all things that are done in the created universe; ... God, after creation, endowed nature with and impressed upon it that capability and power; and ... God merely sustains and preserves that power lest it perish. Consequently, all things that spring forth or are produced and reproduced upon the earth are now ascribed to nature."

> But I replied that nature of itself is not the operative power, but God through nature. And when they asked for proof, I said, "Those who believe the Divine operation to be in every least thing of nature find in very many things they see in the world much more evidence in favor of a God than in favor of nature.

> "For those who find evidence in favor of the Divine operation in every least thing of nature observe attentively the wonderful things that are seen in the production of plants and of animals. In the production of plants, they observe that, from a little seed sown in the ground, there goes forth a root, and from the root a stem, and successively branches, buds, leaves, flowers, and fruits, even to new seeds, just as if the seed knew the order of succession or development by which to renew itself. What rational person can imagine that the sun, which is pure fire, knows this, or that it can impart to its heat and light the power to produce such effects and to have such uses in view? Any man whose reason looks upward, when he sees these things and properly considers them, must conclude that they are from one whose wisdom is infinite, that is from God."

Motivated by this view of the relationship between the Creator and creation, Swedenborg worked among his plants in a spirit of happy cooperation with his God. He had a corner of his garden for experimentation with the propagation of seeds and for growing exotic plants. During his travels to the Continent and to England, he would have encountered many flowers and vegetables that were different from those in Sweden. When he settled down to his own gardening, he was interested in trying some of these out, seeing if they would grow in the northern climate. For example, he ordered chamomile and cucumber seeds from a merchant in Amsterdam, as well as tulip and hyacinth bulbs. We know that he had dogwood trees. It is only conjecture, but a student of Linnaeus's, Pehr Kalm, who went to America in 1748 and particularly to Philadelphia, may have brought the dogwood seedlings back to Swedenborg, as well as the seeds from which he grew watermelons and several other curious plants of the New World.

Swedenborg had a great interest in variety. In the chapter called "Green Growing Things" from her book *The Swedenborg Epic*, Cyriel Sigstedt mentions that among the flowers in the garden were larkspur, scarlet sage, violets, sweet peas, sweet william, flax, and scabiosa. These were only a few of the names she gleaned from notes Swedenborg scribbled in the margin of little almanacs or daybooks, where he recorded the specific pages of manuscripts that he had sent off to the printer. For example, in the notebook for the year 1752, Sigstedt finds mention by Swedenborg of crown artichokes planted in the first box; lemons in the center of the second box, allium, and cypresses, (this may have been a low-growing or creeping variety that would hang over the edge of the box); in the third box three kinds of gillyflowers. In the same year, he notes, "by the currant bush there were old Roses, Marsh Mallows, and Gilliflowers of a curious kind; Parsley and Beets, Spinach and Carrots," and that catmint, bleeding heart, and spurry stocks were planted "by the little tree." The rose garden grew African roses and velvet roses, as well as long-stemmed pinks, Canterbury bells, lilies, rose mallows, and sunflowers. One can imagine the delicious fragrance that hung over the garden, drawn up from all these flowers by the sun.

> [F]or every enjoyment corresponds to an odor and, in the spiritual world may be converted into it. Then the general enjoyment in heaven is sensed as the odor of a garden, varied according to the fragrance of flowers and fruits.
>
> **DIVINE PROVIDENCE, PARAGRAPH 304**

As he worked closely with plants and seeds, Swedenborg was learning at the same time how these natural forms were produced and could demonstrate before our eyes the way spiritual things we cannot see or touch grow and flourish.

> The proliferation of the truths of faith may be compared to the proliferation of seeds in a field or a garden, which may be propagated to myriads of myriads and perpetually. In the Word, "seed" means nothing but truth, "field" means doctrine, and "garden" wisdom. The human mind is like soil, in which the spiritual and natural truths are implanted like seeds and may be endlessly multiplied.
>
> **TRUE CHRISTIAN RELIGION, PARAGRAPH 350**

This concept of a natural garden as correspondential to a spiritual garden is considered in *Heaven and Hell,* paragraph 109:

> How the things in the vegetable kingdom correspond can be seen from many instances, as that little seeds grow into trees, put forth leaves, produce flowers and then fruit, in which again they deposit seed, these things taking place in succession and existing together in an order so wonderful as to be indescribable in a few words. . . . Often when I have been in gardens and have been looking at the trees, fruits, flowers, and plants there, I have recognized their correspondences in heaven.

In 1764, Carl Christopher Gjorwell, librarian of the Royal Library in Stockholm, called on Swedenborg to obtain some of his latest theological books for the library and found Swedenborg in casual attire, among his plants. According to Gjorwell's account (reprinted in "Swedenborg in Stockholm," \ by Olle Hjern), Swedenborg greeted him with a smile and said, "You are going to take a walk here in the garden." When Gjorwell said that he had actually come for the honor of meeting Swedenborg and for additional volumes of his writings to complete the holdings of the Royal Library, his host graciously invited Gjorwell into the house.

But after they had dealt with the books, they went out to see the garden. Like most gardeners, Swedenborg evidently took great pleasure in having others enjoy his garden. While walking among the trees and flowers, Swedenborg began to talk about some of the spiritual ideas that were in the books that Gjorwell was to take away with him. And perhaps Swedenborg spoke also about the spiritual truths and beauties contained in the correspondences of his garden.

That plants have correspondences or meanings beyond their natural forms should not surprise us. We speak even today of the language of the flowers, although we don't actually employ it very often, except perhaps on Valentine's Day when a lover may send red roses to a sweetheart. Various colored flowers still have various meanings, like red for love and white for purity. Epithets are attached to trees and shrubs. The oak is strong and long enduring— hearts of oak. The weeping willow embodies grief, and we talk of a bereaved person wearing the willow. Yews were planted in graveyards as symbolic of death. The ancients believed that the spheres of plants were part of their healing or sickening properties. And all these myths and meanings come from a spiritual origin.

> [T]he particular things in nature are like tunics, sheaths, and clothing which encircle spiritual things, and proximately produce effects correspondent to the end designed by God the Creator.
>
> **TRUE CHRISTIAN RELIGION, PARAGRAPH 695:6**

Here are some examples of this. The Greeks, who had some half-forgotten knowledge of correspondences, gave crowns of laurel to those who excelled in skill and intelligence. This came from the laurel's spiritual meaning as the affection or love of certain truths put into use or action. Fragrant and lovely flowers have always been used as decorations for weddings because flowers represent the state of a couple before marriage and can be compared to the joy of the bride and the bridegroom. A bridal bouquet of flowers was, once at least, a symbol of future fruitfulness, the hoped-for blessing of children. But more interiorly, it is a sign that the marriage will bear heavenly fruit in a union of love and wisdom. Often, the bride carries roses. The rose has always been associated with eternal love, and beds of roses correspond to the beautiful things of heavenly life. "Each rose becomes a plane on which are formed interior deliciousnesses to eternity," we are told in the *Spiritual Diary*, paragraph 6110.

Every part of a plant—seed, root, branch, leaf, flower, and fruit—has a meaning important to the development of the human being toward heavenly life. Swedenborg explains these at length in the volumes of his theological writings. Every plant also has a specific spiritual meaning: The palm tree is the joy of heart that comes from seeking spiritual good; the apple tree, the joy of heart from natural good. Leeks, onions, and garlic are of the lowest natural or sensuous level of a person. In his books, Swedenborg did not catalog the correspondence of every known plant or even every plant that he had in his garden, although all would have their individual meanings. His particular endeavor was to unfold the spiritual meaning of the Bible, and so he deals primarily with those trees, herbs, flowers, and weeds that we find in the Old and New Testaments. For he knew that in the garden of the Lord's Word are the seeds of truth that we need to plant in the soil of our minds so that good affections can blossom in our hearts and bear fruit in our lives. We need to be a garden as well as a gardener.

> A person is like a tree, which first grows up from a seed into a
> shoot, and when it increases in height puts forth branches and
> from these stems, and clothes itself continually with leaves;
> and when it comes to maturity, which takes place in its middle
> age, puts forth flowers, and produces fruits. In each one, it

places seeds, which being cast into the earth, as into a womb, grow up into similar trees and thus into a garden. *And if you are willing to believe it* [italics mine], the same garden remains with the person after death; he dwells in it, and is delighted daily with the sight of it, and with the use of its fruits.

THE CORONIS, PARAGRAPH 7

At my suggestion, this passage from *Coronis* was read at the resurrection service for Laddie, my cousin and close childhood friend. Her physical death came at the beginning of February just a few days short of her natural birthday. A week or two earlier, I wrote about Laddie in my journal:

1999

JANUARY 17

Some of Laddie's care-givers seem concerned that she isn't facing the reality of her imminent death from cancer, because she is ordering seeds and planning a summer vegetable garden. Confined to a wheelchair as she is, right now the garden in her mind is her life. The promise of the coming spring, her bulbs blooming, growing greens for salads are all symbolic of a return to vigor and health. We know that this will not happen in this world, and she may too—unconsciously. But it is better to plan for life than to dwell morbidly on death. The garden she is anticipating in the spring is not only the one that she can see out the window; symbolically, correspondentially, she is planting in her life those affections for truth and beauty that have consequences for her eternity.

A day or two before she died, Laddie said sadly to her brother, "I won't see the daffodils bloom." But I believe she will, that her garden will remain with her after death and delight her every day with the love of it.

One of my favorite things to think about is that all the while that we are growing our gardens here, we are also planting spiritual gardens. And everyone's spiritual garden will be different, "for everything good and true is called a garden, with variation depending on the person who tends it" (*Arcana Coelestia*, paragraph 225).

Three years to the day after my husband Bruce died, I wrote this entry in my journal:

1995
MAY 27

As I pushed the lawnmower through the lush grass late this afternoon and into the early evening, I thought a lot about my husband; for mowing the lawn was always Bruce's part of the yard work, as weeding was mine. What we loved was working on our property together. I wish he could be back here on earth for just this twilight hour and take a stroll with me around our gardens. The wildflower garden is rather faded now and past its prime, but the herb garden outside the kitchen door is like a picture by Tasha Tudor. Around the side of the house, I have started a rose garden, and the Carefree Beauty bush, which he never saw, is abloom with fragrant, old-fashioned pink roses. In the front rock garden, the Saponaria, one of his favorites, is glowing in the last of the light.

The gardens that he is enjoying in his new life may be much more beautiful than this, but this was ours. My most ardent hope is that someday we will live and work together again in our own spiritual garden in heaven.

*Fall is a season of fruitfulness and harvest, but it is
also when the new buds form on the trees.*

On the Fall of the Year

SEPTEMBER/OCTOBER/NOVEMBER

EVEN IF SOMETHING IS LEFT UNDONE, EVERYONE MUST TAKE TIME
TO SIT STILL AND WATCH THE LEAVES TURN.
ELIZABETH LAURENCE

By late August, though it seems summer still, there are signs that fall is coming. The early mornings are misty, and the grass stays dewy until noon. From all this moisture comes a spontaneous generation of mushrooms and toadstools; fantastic growths explode out of damp ground and rotting wood. Most days are hot and sticky, but along will come a day when there's no hint of humidity, and the air is so clear that all the leaves shine as if they were polished. The warblers begin passing through on their long trip south; Queen Anne's lace and toadflax give way along the roadsides to goldenrod and pale asters.

I love the fall. For me, with my long orientation to school, it has always seemed like the beginning of a new year. As a child, I always had new clothes, new books, and an apple from the orchard in my pocket for recess. Even after all these years, and now in retirement from teaching, I still find September full of excitement and promise.

1986

SEPTEMBER 18

This last week I spent several afternoons after school in the wildflower garden clearing the paths of unwanted growth so that we can enjoy walking in the autumn woods of our own backyard. The garden has white clumps of snakeroot, the side fence is hung with wild clematis, or virgin's bower. Soon the blossoms will turn to wispy gray plumes and take on the appearance that gives it the English name, old-man's beard.

1995

SEPTEMBER 24

The berries on the dogwood are ripe. I wake in the morning to the sound of squirrels chewing up the seeds inside the red husks. The squirrels are entertaining to watch, balancing on the thin branches or hanging upside down by their hind feet to feed, using their tails as auxiliary props.

Among the first leaves to color in the autumn, the dogwoods change during September from a scarlet and green mix to a deep carmine, framing clusters of bright red berries. When the berries have been eaten by the wild things and the leaves have dropped in October, the gray buds emerge on the slightly upturned twigs, looking like tiny Cornish pasties. Fall is a season of fruitfulness and harvest, but it is also when the new buds form on the trees.

In April and May, the FLOWERING DOGWOODS are angel trees with bright wings reflecting the sun or floating in the light of a full moon. The *Cornus florida*, of which I now have six in the wild garden, were transplanted as seedlings from other places in the yard. They look wonderfully natural among the other trees, for that is how they grow in the woods of southeastern Pennsylvania. The opening flowers are greenish, but as they spread wide, the petals (actually bracts) become bright white, creamy, or sometimes faintly pink. The four large bracts, nicked with umber, form a broad cross around the true flower cluster. The summer-green leaves are oval, the veins following the smooth edges toward the tip.

Peterson's guide tells me that the powdered bark of the dogwood was once used as toothpaste, as a substitute for quinine, and, when mixed with iron sulfate, as a black ink. The wood is hard and close-grained, and was manufactured in earlier times into mallets, handles for tools, golf club heads, shuttles, and bobbins. The bark of the roots produces a scarlet dye. There is obviously a red principle in the tree that comes out in the twigs and berries, and in the natural pinkish bloom of some trees. It was the pinkest of these that were propagated and used to graft the red flowering dogwoods that are sold by nurseries.

There is another kind of dogwood in the garden, which I have tentatively identified as a STIFF DOGWOOD. I don't know why it is given this name, as the small tree is droopy, rather than rigid. But I remember similar ones growing in the swampy area on the farm, and the stiff dogwood is supposed to like wet places. The leaves are similar to the flowering dogwood, but paler on the underside, more sharply tipped, and on longer red-hued stems. In the fall, they do not have the same brilliant red hue. The stiff dogwood also blooms a week or so later than the *Cornus florida*. The flowers are small, in round-topped, fuzzy-looking clusters, white to cream-colored. The berries, which develop in clusters like the flowers, are blue, coming August to September.

1990

SEPTEMBER 28

A chipmunk is busy harvesting acorns from the pin oak by the porch. He scurries up the trunk and down, his cheeks bulging, scampers across the patio, over the lawn, and into his hole at the corner of the herb garden.

1995

SEPTEMBER 25

There are a lot of acorns this year, enough for everyone, but the jays are arguing over the abundance. Many birds certainly seem to be on the selfish and combative side, like jays and crows. Even robins, for all their endearing nesting and nurturing habits, battle fiercely over mates and territory. I do admire the courteous cardinals; they have unobtrusive good manners, and their monogamous ways are almost moral.

About ten years ago, an OAK volunteered in the west corner of the garden where two fences meet. It is a sturdy young tree now, at least twenty feet high, but still a youth as oaks go. I suppose that it is probably a pin oak, as there is a mature tree nearby. Its leaves are definitely in the "lobed with bristle tips" category. Rutherford Platt, in *A Pocket Guide to Trees*, calls this the black oak group, and George

Petrides of the Peterson guide series calls it the red oak group. Of all the trees that are difficult to identify, an oak seems to be the hardest. I'm told that even professionals have trouble because of all the species and the variants. I'm going for a subgroup called the scarlet-pin oak group *Quercus coccinea* or *Quercus palustris,* or some variation of one or the other. I read in both tree guides that the acorn is the most positive clue to what kind of oak a tree is, but this tree has not had acorns yet, so I still have it under surveillance. No native woodland is complete without an oak of some kind, and I am delighted to have this one in my tree garden.

When there are only a few flowers, as in the autumn, I become more aware of the trees and the shrubs. I am reminded of something that Swedenborg wrote in *Conjugial Love* about a garden in the spiritual world. He once observed a party of visitors, people newly arrived from earth, who were being shown around a certain heavenly community. The angel guide asked if they would like to see the Prince's garden, which was by far the most magnificent in the society. The visitors responded with enthusiasm, but were disappointed when they got to the entrance and all they saw beyond was a single great tree. The angel said, "Go closer and your eyes will be opened, and you will see the garden."

Then, they saw many trees in a continuous circle or spiral, with fruit-laden branches bending in toward the great central tree. The leaves shone with the light, which fell between the trees like shafts of gold. Among the trees were places to sit, bowers formed of intertwining branches. Here and there, the trees opened out into lawns and flowerbeds. The visitors exclaimed in delight.

> The angel rejoiced at hearing this, and said, "The gardens in our heaven are all representative forms or types of states of heavenly blessedness in their origin; and it is because an influx of these states of blessedness uplifted your minds that you perceived a model of heaven. But those that do not receive this influx see these paradises as nothing but a woodsy scene.
>
> **CONJUGIAL LOVE, PARAGRAPH 13**

I do not pretend to have a garden that is close to being a model of heaven at any time of year, but I know that the way I see my garden is different from the way most any visitor sees it. For example, when I take friends through the garden after the spring bloom is gone, I know that they are disappointed. They can't envision as I do the forget-me-nots and the daffodils, the dogwoods hung with garlands of white blossoms. They see only what is there, the summer green of ferns, the foliage overhead—"a woodsy scene."

It is said that beauty is in the eye of the beholder. How true. That is why angels can see a whole heavenly garden in a single tree, and why I find things to enjoy in my garden through all the seasons. The spring garden has the beauty of flowers, but in the summer, autumn, and winter, the garden is mainly a garden of trees.

It is interesting how many heavenly gardens, as described by Swedenborg, are composed of trees, and especially fruit-bearing trees. We learn by reading him that the process of fruiting corresponds to the things that we do in this world with our minds, hearts, and bodies to make life eternally worthwhile for ourselves and for other people. These good things are the first fruits of our land that we offer up to heaven—gifts given by God that return to God. And from this comes the happiness of the spiritual gardener.

I am delighted that some of the trees here in my natural garden fruit and provide a banquet for wild birds, squirrels, rabbits, mice, and a host of other creatures so small or shy that I usually fail to notice them. By far the most prolific tree is the native *Morus rubra*, or RED MULBERRY, with ropes of pulpy berrylike fruits that ripen from red to purple-black. In mid-June, the mulberry tree in the wild garden and the one in the backyard are full of diners: cardinals, robins, mockingbirds, sparrows, jays, and boat-tailed grackles. Often they fly back and forth between the two trees as if trying to decide which berries have the best flavor. And on the ground are starlings, cowbirds, more robins, and the squirrels that aren't up in the tree. Actually, I think the squirrels prefer the dead ripe fruit fallen on the ground because it ferments in the heat and sometimes makes them a little tipsy.

A mulberry tree grows to a good height if given the air space, although the branches tend to droop, which brings it back down to earth. The trunk has reddish-brown bark with ridges, and it often divides near the ground into two or three trunks. The leaves are shiny green on top, paler and somewhat hairy underneath, heart-shaped or lobed, the edges finely saw-toothed. This is not the mulberry whose leaves were fed to silkworms in colonial times, that was the white mulberry imported from Asia.

Originally, there were two CHOKECHEERY trees—also heavy fruit-producers—in the garden. The birds loved the seedy cherries, which was fine, but unfortunately, the leaves were like Pablum for newly hatched tent caterpillars. The plague of creepy-crawlies seems to come in waves. How well I remember them dropping on my head as I walked to and from elementary school under the chokecherry trees along the road. Horrible things! Our local Boys Club launched a campaign, and boys won prizes for collecting the thick, white webs before the eggs hatched out. After that, the caterpillars subsided for a while, but by the eighties, they were on the increase again. That was when we decided to take the trees down, for our sake, but more to placate the neighbors who were beginning to be most unhappy about the caterpillars.

In the fall of 1988 I wrote in my journal:

1988

NOVEMBER 13

Yesterday afternoon the crew from Tree Down came to put down the two chokecherry trees in the wild garden. The one tree on the far side of the garden hung out over the electric and phone lines. Two years ago, in a storm, the tree was hit by lightning and a big branch fell down on the wires and cut off power to half the street. When we saw how charred the branch was, we felt lucky a fire hadn't started. For safety reasons, it was probably best that tree came down anyway. But the other chokecherry was a big, straight-growing tree, and I feel a little sad this morning to see only the stump. Too late now, of course, but I do have a sense of regret. It's hard to cut down a living tree just because its leaves are food for caterpillars. That is, after all, the way of creation. Who are we to try and arrange nature to suit our convenience and make things more pleasant for ourselves with no regard for the greater ecological picture or the wisdom of the Divine?

> What wonders do we see in worms, the meanest creatures in the animal kingdom! They know how to get food from the juice of the leaves suited to them, and afterward at the appointed time to invest themselves with a covering and enter as it were into a womb, and thus hatch offspring of their own kind. Some are first turned into nymphs and chrysalides, spinning threads about themselves; and this travail being over they come forth clad with a different body, furnished with wings with which they fly in the air as in their heaven, and celebrate marriages and lay eggs and provide posterity for themselves.
>
> **HEAVEN AND HELL, PARAGRAPH 108:2**

In this poetic passage, Swedenborg points out the workings of God in even the lower natural forms of the animal kingdom. But perhaps it is enough, once we appreciate the wonder of God, not to have to also appreciate the tent caterpillars.

The crowning glory among the trees in my wild garden was an AMERICAN ELM, *Ulmus americana*, and we discovered it by cutting down the big chokecherry. Apparently, the elm is a one-of-a-kind tree, never living in groves of its own species, but in the company of other kinds of trees. For years it was crowded in, hard pressed by the cherry to one side and a Norway maple and the mulberry to the other. It was the foreman of the tree crew who said, "Hey, I think you have an American elm out there. You'll be able to tell for sure next spring when the leaves come out."

Because of its warped childhood, our elm would never be a perfect specimen, but in the spring, against the open sky revealed by the demise of the cherry, we saw the familiar fountain shape of this lovely native tree. The leaves, even then, were so far above our heads that we could not use them as a means of proving the tree's identification, but the squirrels have a curious habit of nipping off the tender ends of the twigs of the elm and letting them drop to the ground. I found the leaf clusters scattered on the path below the tree where I could easily pick one up and examine it. The leaves were double-toothed, dark green, smooth on top, and a little rough underneath. And, yes, there was the typical American elm off-center symmetry, formed by a graceful curvature of the leaf's spine from a lopsided base. This tendency to be askew is repeated in the buds, which don't come at the ends of the twigs, but jut off at an angle, and then the twig follows suit, producing a zigzag pattern, growing first in one direction and then in another. Perhaps this is what gives the branches such a graceful fall.

Unfortunately, the elm tree did not enjoy good health in the last years. The bark sloughed off on one side, and huge shelf fungi, orange and brown, grew near the base and up the trunk. Dutch elm disease is carried by a fungus, but elms that I have seen affected by that disease don't sport these flamboyant, fan-shaped fungi. Perhaps the one condition has followed the other. The only thing to do for Dutch elm disease is to cut down the tree and burn it, but I haven't the heart to do it. There is no symptom of general withering, although there are some dead branches. I thought I would wait until I was forced to admit that the whole tree was sick to death, and then I'd deal with it. But in the meantime, I hoped maybe my affection would keep the tree alive.

My love was not as strong as the ravages of wind and rain from Hurricane Floyd. In September 1999, the elm was torn up by the roots and neatly laid to rest in the backyard. It missed the arbor by the herb garden and only grazed the chestnut tree in its fall through the wild garden, although it flattened a section of the privet hedge. The tree was sawed up, chipped up, and most carried away in a few hours. I feel that I have lost an old friend and realize more poignantly than ever that there is death as well as life in the garden.

Still standing in the center of my garden is a buckeye or HORSE CHESTNUT. I think it is *Aesculus hippocastanum*. It popped up in the middle of the mayapples and forget-me-nots one spring about five years ago. The planter may have been a squirrel or a child, or even myself emptying some shiny red-brown nuts out my pockets after a walk in the Pennypack woods. The chestnuts are so beautiful that I never like to just throw them in the trash. Irresistible to pick up after they fall out of their prickly hedgehog husks, they are a sensual delight to smooth over and over with your fingers. My children used to keep a collection from year to year. Some of them had been hollowed out by their father to make little leather-like containers with the rough tan eye patch as a lid, or carved into tiny jack-o'-lanterns.

The tree is still only a sapling of about twelve feet. Someday it could be as high as seventy-five feet, a really respectable tree if I give it place by a hard cutting-back of the sprawly mulberry and the privet (which wouldn't do either any harm.) Its trunk bark is gray-brown and somewhat scaly. The lower branches tend to undulate up and down and up again. The leaves splay out like a palm-leaf fan, with from five to seven or more wedge-shaped, toothed leaflets.

Last year, the tree bloomed for the first time. In May, there was one torch-shaped cluster of yellowish blossoms. When the petals fell, it reminded me of the line by A. E. Housman. After my chestnut cast its single flambeaux, I watched eagerly to see if it would set little nuts in bristly cases, but it did not. Perhaps it was just too immature to fruit, for this year there were both blossoms and nuts. My daughter Rachel picked up six chestnuts around the base of the tree and put them on the bookcase by the old farmhouse clock. Here they remind us that time passing is more than hours: it is coming to maturity and bearing fruit.

Several years ago, I wrote in my journal about how pleasant and peaceful our little plot of woods is in the fall, considering that we have neighbors on three sides. It seems somehow removed from the world, although it is in the world. And perhaps that is part of the charm.

1994

OCTOBER 5

Early October is a somnolent time in the garden. The bright leaf colors haven't emerged yet, and the flowers are over for another season. With no work to be done, it is pleasant to sit and ruminate in the soft autumn hush.

Usually, by the middle of October, we have had a frost and count the next warm spell as Indian summer. Somewhere, sometime, I heard someone speculating on Indian summer—why it is called that? One of the theories was that, like "Indian giving," it doesn't last; another was that the bright colors of the foliage are like Indian war paint. Or, perhaps, it was in this respite before the cold really set in that the Indians prepared for winter by gathering in food supplies, smoking meat or fish, and feasting before the lean times. The first Thanksgiving—a sharing of bounty between the pilgrim settlers and the Native Americans—may have been held in one of these warm spells. No mean wind stirring, no brilliance to the air; time seems to hang in hazy suspension before the wild geese fly.

By late October, we have been to the Pennypack Trust for bird food and have put up the feeders. In the wildflower garden, only a few late spears of goldenrod are hanging on in the sunny patch by the fence on the west side. The flowers and weeds have seeded and begun to die away. The afternoon light slanting through the yellow leaves overhead picks up a few bright berries on the Solomon's plume, lights the red-bronze of Epimedium, and shows off the autumn garb of some of the shrubs.

The bush with the fleshy, round, red berries is a SWAMP-FLY HONEYSUCKLE. The fruits remind me of currants, though I have never heard of anyone eating them. The oblong leaves, which don't have much autumn coloring, give it the second part of its botanical name, *Lonicera oblongifolia*, but it is the flowers that identify it as a honeysuckle. They are smaller than the white and ivory blooms of the climbing honeysuckle vine that hold a drop of sweet liquid at the base of their trumpets; however, the form of the flower is the same—hand-shaped, the palm petal divided into four digits with a longer petal at the bottom like an opposable thumb. It is a large, old shrub and provides a good screen on the east side, where there is no fence. The bushes grow thickly around here in scrubby woods, especially in swampy areas or along a stream bank.

In the back of my garden, just this side of the new fence, is a MOCK ORANGE, *Philadelphus coronarius*. A long time ago, when the property line was not so rigid and the place where our house stands was a field, this bush may have been planted at the corner of the neighboring lawn. It's a sprawly sort of shrub with undistinguished foliage, but admired for its fragrant white blossoms that come in late May or June after most shrubs have stopped blooming. In days past, these flowers were sometimes used to crown the country bride here in the north, where true orange blossoms were not available or very expensive.

1997

NOVEMBER 1

After the most beautiful month of October, the wildflower garden has gone into late-fall mode. Some dull autumn days make you feel more melancholy than nostalgic, but today, in spite of the rain, the color out back is still quite cheerful—the tiny, bright-orange leaves of the spirea, the golden-yellow of the spicebush, and red-pink fire of the burning bush.

The SPICEBUSH, so common to the woods around Bryn Athyn, is a shrub that I associate with my childhood. When we walked or played in the woods, we often broke a twig off to chew for the spicy flavor. And there was nothing better for roasting a hot dog or marshmallow over a campfire than a long wand cut from the spicebush. I have heard that the twigs and leaves can be used for brewing a kind of tea, and the red berries powdered and used as a spice, but I have never tried it. The buds, like tiny green balls along the twigs and branches, open in March to fuzzy, yellow, aromatic flowers.

They are not spectacular, but nevertheless, they are exciting to see in the early garden and to add to a bouquet of daffodils in the house. In the fall, the smooth, elliptical leaves turn a golden-yellow, lighting up the understory of the woodland.

Against the fence between my wild garden and the western neighbor's backyard is a BURNING BUSH, *Euonymus atropurpureus*, which does seem to be on fire in the autumn. The pointed, oval leaves that branch out in stiff pairs from the ridged twigs turn flame-red or glow with the bright pink of embers. Then, too, the fruits—which resemble bittersweet, but have a bright red inner berry with a purple husk around it—shoot off like sparks. Where the berries drop in the fall, the spring brings up a crop of tiny seedlings. These berries are not supposed to be much sought after by birds (and they are rumored to be poisonous to children). But this fall, I saw birds among the berries twice: once sparrows, and again a whole flock of young robins.

1986

NOVEMBER 6
Most of the color in the trees is gone, but the Norway maples have just turned their quite astonishing autumn hue. The "old gold" trees, I used to call them. By 4:30 in the afternoon, the golden light of the westering sun is streaming through the yellow branches and creating a heavenly radiance in the wild garden.

NOVEMBER 8
Even on a dull day, the Norway maples seem to be full of sunlight. The silent drifting down of their yellow leaves reminds me of some lines from a poem by Gerard Manley Hopkins addressing a young girl:

> *Margaret, are you grieving*
> *Over golden groves unleaving? . . .*
> *Ah! as the heart grows older*
> *It will come to such sights colder.*

But I haven't—come colder, that is. The falling of the Norway maple leaves always brings on a late-autumn sadness.

Well established along the back property line when I began the garden was a NORWAY MAPLE, *Acer platanoides*. There was another at the west front edge of the garden; it has since died and been taken down. This species of maple tends to wrap its roots around itself and cut off the sap supply—a sort of botanical suicide. So although the tree grows quickly and often reaches quite a height, it doesn't usually live to a ripe old age.

Two distinguishing characteristics of the Norway maple are the milky sap in the leaf stalks and the upward tilt of the seed wings. In the late summer, the green pods come whirling down from the branches like tiny helicopters. Our children used to retrieve them and throw them up in the air to watch them come spinning down again, or split the pods in the center and attach them to their noses by the sticky juice. "Witch's noses," my husband used to call them.

I was amused to read of this tree in the *Peterson Field Guide to Trees and Shrubs* as "occasionally spreading from plantings to upland fields and hedgerows." *Occasionally* is the understatement of the plant world. Every year, the Norway maple sends out a winged army, and the next spring, the tiny saplings rise up like paratroopers turned into infantry. It is constant warfare between the gardener and the threatened encroachment. A professor of biology, who was a friend and colleague, once saw a Norway sapling allowed to flourish in the wildflower garden and said: "You want to get rid of that bloodsucker. Terrible trees, nothing grows under them." It's true, they are gross feeders. I did get rid of it, deciding, on his advice, that two was enough for one garden. And if I really wanted another, there would be about twenty opportunities coming along next year.

Norway maples were brought from Europe and planted along streets and by houses. The heavy foliage makes them excellent summer shade trees, but in the autumn, this creates a tremendous raking problem when the leaves fall on the lawn or the street. But in the late fall, they are so beautiful that I forgive the Norway maples for everything.

Another tree that colors very late in the fall is the JAPANESE MAPLE. The small, deeply cut leaves with five tapering points turn red and yellow and then maroon, like embers holding the last of the heat. Although this maple is an ornamental rather than a woodland tree, all of the trees in the garden are wild in the sense that they grew from seed where they stand or volunteered somewhere else and were transplanted. The Japanese maple in the wild garden is third-generation. It came from a seedling that grew under the tree near the house, which came from a seedling that grew under Bruce's mother's tree over on Alnwick Road. It's interesting to think of trees having generations. The bark of the young tree is smooth and gray; the bark of its mother has the dark, rough patches of age. The mother tree is not large as maples grow, only about thirty feet, up to the eaves of our house. Its branches spread out laterally, and layer above layer of leaves form a canopy over the patio that effectively keeps out all but the heaviest rain. On a hot summer day, it is delightful to lie in the hammock under the shade and look up into the leaves like clusters of little green stars against the sky.

1987

NOVEMBER 8

The world has fallen into a melancholy November mood—a warm, wistful morning of weak sunlight with mist round the edges. Despite the mild day, I can feel the garden hunkering down for winter. On our walk around Cairncrest this afternoon, Bruce said, "Do you realize that in less than three months we'll be out looking for snowdrops?"

1988

NOVEMBER 19

The light is like pewter. Wedges of gray geese with their strange, wild cries fly like arrowheads across the gray sky.

NOVEMBER 26

Except for the oaks, most of the leaves have fallen and the branches are bare. We spent part of the Thanksgiving weekend raking the yard and spreading the leaves on the paths of the wildflower garden, bedding down for the long sleep.

*The American holly is a common understory tree of our
native woods that comes into its glory in December.*

EPILOGUE

DECEMBER

WHEN IT IS TOO COLD FOR COMFORT, THE SUN-FILLED
GARDEN PROMISES THAT WINTER WILL BE BRIEF.
NORMAN KENT JOHNSON

1997

DECEMBER 9

A real winter morning, temperature about 30 degrees, frost on the ground, a Currier-and-Ives-print sky. In the early light, the privet hedge looks all silvery-lavender on top where the leaves still hold to the twigs. Below, the branches and stems are bare.

The year in the wild garden has wound down to dormant December. We look to the evergreens to relieve the drabness. Of all the evergreens, I love best the tall WHITE PINES. Three were planted in the corner of the property fifty years ago, and they now tower skyward well over a hundred feet. The tree in the wild garden is an offspring of one of these. It began when one of the flat seed cases slipped from a slender cone, germinated, and became a tiny sprout with a whorl of soft green needles. Now the tree is no longer a baby, and although still small and scrawny, quite recognizable as a white pine *(Pinus strobus)* with lateral branches, thick twigs ending in bunches of five-cluster needles.

Then there is the RED CEDAR, *Juniperus virginiana*, which grows all along the eastern seaboard from Maine to Georgia and west into Texas. It likes dry soil and old fields. On a drive from Bryn Athyn to New Hope through Bucks County, there is ample evidence of red cedars. From a rise in the Windy Bush Road, looking out toward the Delaware River, you can see a band of them across the abandoned farmland, standing out blue-green in the brown winter landscape. The foliage is bristling with sharp little needles, blue-green in color. Even if my tree is single, I like being part of this natural phenomenon. The cedar foliage is bristling with sharp little needles; the small round fruits are blue-black when ripe and are consumed by birds and other wildlife, and sometimes by people as flavoring. Because the bark is dry and shreddy, it was once used as tinder by campers to start a warming fire. Rose-brown and aromatic, the heart wood is built into chests and closets for its odor, which repels wool-eating moths and keeps safe the coats and blankets.

The most magical time in the December garden is after the first snowfall. I wrote in my journal:

1985

DECEMBER 5

The first snow of the season began last night while we were in choir rehearsal. We came out of the church to whiteness on the lawns and wetness on walks and roads. This morning there is an inch or two of snow clinging to everything, and the light flakes are still falling with a wonderful quietness.

That early snow was unusual. We always hope for snow by Christmas, but rarely get it. Instead we have to depend on the inner joy of the holy day to provide its own brightness. December is the darkest month of the year. And the world was in the deepest state of spiritual darkness when Christ came to bring light—the bright and morning star.

1989

DECEMBER 25

It is a cold Christmas morning. Only eleven degrees above zero at 7:15 when Bruce drew my attention tot he beautiful sunrise. A lovely start to a special day. "This is the day that the Lord has made." Although that is true of every morning, it seems especially true of Christmas Day. As it says in Psalm 118, "We will rejoice and be glad in it."

In the garden are the holly and the ivy of the traditional carol, and the pointed fronds of the hardy Christmas fern. The AMERICAN HOLLY, *Ilex opaca,* is a common understory tree of our native woods, rising in a kind of triangular spire, if one finds a good specimen. It comes into its glory in December. It is so prized for Christmas decorations that many of the trees have been mutilated beyond recognition for the spiked evergreen leaves and the red berries. The two that I have in the wild garden have rich, green, leathery foliage, but no berries. Hollies divide into sexes and these are both obviously male trees. A little disappointing, because the red berries hang on tight through the cold and would give color to the winter garden.

1990

DECEMBER 29

The temperature held about 34 degrees Fahrenheit all night. This morning the world is full of fog and the stealthy sound of melting snow. So the old year drags to a gray close. A new year and a new beginning are only days away.

Many non-gardeners think of winter as death. But gardeners know that, although things may look moribund, life is still there. The buds that hold the flower and the leaf are set on tree and shrub. Energy is packed up tight in root and bulb. The seed is in the ground ready to spring into action. Everything in the vegetable kingdom is at the ready, waiting for "the force that through the green fuse drives the flower" as the poet Dylan Thomas wrote. All it takes is the right amount of earth rotation, the right amount of natural and spiritual sunshine. Nature sleeps to waken; the garden dies to come alive again.

And by late January the snowdrops will be blooming once again.

Take a flower home, plant and nurture it, and
it will survive, multiply, and fill the earth.

PLANTS IN THE WILD GARDEN

IT IS APPARENT THAT NO LIFETIME IS LONG ENOUGH IN WHICH
TO EXPLORE THE RESOURCES OF A FEW SQUARE YARDS OF GROUND.
ALICE COATES

SOURCES AND RESOURCES

Barber, Peter, and C. E. Lucas-Phillips. 1975. *The Trees Around Us*, illus. Delia Delderfield. Chicago: Follett Publishing Co.

Berger, Terry. 1984. *Garden Proverbs*. Philadelphia: Running Press.

Dole, George F., and Robert H. Kirven. 1992. *A Scientist Explores Spirit, A Compact Biography of Emanuel Swedenborg with Key Concepts of Swedenborg's Theology*. West Chester, Penna.: Swedenborg Foundation.

Freeman, Margaret. 1976. *The Unicorn Tapestries*. New York: The Metropolitan Museum of Art.

The Gardener's Notebook: A Personal Journal. 1983. Philadelphia: Running Press.

Gottscho, Samuel. 1960. *A Pocket Guide to Wildflowers: How to Identify and Enjoy Them*. New York: Washington Square Press.

Hjern, Olle. 1988. "Swedenborg in Stockholm." *Emanuel Swedenborg, A Continuing Vision*, ed. Robin Larsen. New York: Swedenborg Foundation.

Holden, Edith. 1977. *The Country Diary of an Edwardian Lady*. New York: Holt, Rinehart and Winston.

J. C. L. S. 1867. "Description of Swedenborg's House and Garden," *Intellectual Repository*. London. Reprinted in pages 491-493 in Cyriel Sigstedt, *The Swedenborg Epic: Life and Works of Emanuel Swedenborg*. New York: Bookman Assoc. 1952.

Johnson, Marjorie P., comp., and Montague Free, ed. 1953. *The Concise Encyclopedia of Favorite Flowers*. Garden City, N.Y.: The American Garden Guild and Doubleday & Co.

Olds, Charles Louis. [no date]. *Flora's Clock*. Unpublished manuscript.

Parker, Helen, ed. 1996. *Perennials*, Eyewitness Garden Handbooks. Boston: DK Publishing.

Parsons, Frances Theodora. 1927. *How to Know the Ferns: A Guide to the Names, Haunts, and Habits of our Common Ferns*. Marion Satterlee and Alice J. Smith, illus. New York: Charles Scribner's Sons.

Peterson, Roger Tory, and Margaret McKenny. 1968. *A Field Guide to Wildflowers of Northeastern and Northcentral North America.* R. T. Peterson, illus. Boston: Houghton Mifflin Co.

Petrides, George A. 1972. *Trees and Shrubs,* second ed. Peterson Field Guide Series. George A. Petrides and Roger Tory Peterson, illus. Boston, New York: Houghton Mifflin Co.

Platt, Rutherford. 1972. *A Pocket Guide to Trees.* Margaret Cosgrove, illus. New York: Pocket Books.

Sigstedt, Cyriel Odhner. 1952. *The Swedenborg Epic: Life and Works of Emanuel Swedenborg.* New York: Bookman Assoc.

Stokoe, W. J., comp. 1967. *The Observer's Book of Wild Flowers.* London: Frederick Warne & Co.

Swedenborg, Emanuel. 1995–1998. *Arcana Coelestia.* 2nd ed. Translated by John F. Potts. West Chester, Penna.: The Swedenborg Foundation.

———. 1998. *Conjugial Love.* 2nd ed. Translated by Samuel S. Warren. West Chester, Penna.: The Swedenborg Foundation.

———. 1996. "Coronis." In *Posthumous Theological Works,* vol. 1. 2nd ed. Translated by John Whitehead. West Chester, Penna.: The Swedenborg Foundation.

———. 1996. *Divine Love and Wisdom.* 2nd ed. Translated by John C. Ager. West Chester, Penna.: Swedenborg Foundation.

———. 1996. *Divine Providence.* 2nd ed. Translated by William Wunsch. West Chester, Penna.: The Swedenborg Foundation.

———. 1996. *Heaven and Hell.* Translated by John C. Ager. West Chester, Penna.: The Swedenborg Foundation.

———. 1986. *Journal of Dreams, 1743–1744.* Translated by J.J.G. Wilkinson. Commentary by Wilson Van Dusen. New York: Swedenborg Foundation.

———. 1883. *Spiritual Diary.* George Bush and Rev. John H. Smithson, trans. London: James Speir.

———. 1996. *True Christian Religion.* 2nd edition. Translated by John C. Ager. West Chester, Penna.: Swedenborg Foundation.

Vesey-Fitzgerald, Brian. 1957. *The Ladybird Book of British Wild Flowers.* Rowland and Edith Hilder, illus. Loughborough, England: Wills & Hepworth.